D0586401

THE WOMAN
WHO TICKLED
TOO MUCH

THE WOMAN
WHO TICKLED
TOO MUCH

AND OTHER INCREDIBLE STORIES
FROM INSIDE BRITAIN'S LAW COURTS

JONATHAN HERRING

**Prentice Hall
is an imprint of**

Harlow, England • London • New York • Boston • San Francisco • Toronto
Sydney • Tokyo • Singapore • Hong Kong • Seoul • Taipei • New Delhi
Cape Town • Madrid • Mexico City • Amsterdam • Munich • Paris • Milan

PEARSON EDUCATION LIMITED
Edinburgh Gate
Harlow CM20 2JE
Tel: +44 (0)1279 623623
Fax: +44 (0)1279 431059
Website: www.pearsoned.co.uk

First published in Great Britain in 2009

ISBN: 978-0-273-72325-7

British Library Cataloguing-in-Publication Data
A catalogue record for this book is available from the British Library

Library of Congress Cataloging-in-Publication Data
A catalog record for this book is available from the Library of Congress

10 9 8 7 6 5 4 3 2 1
13 12 11 10 09

Design by Julie Martin
Illustrations by Nick Redeyoff
Typeset in 12/16.5pt Ehrhardt MT Rg by 30
Printed and bound in Great Britain by Henry Ling Ltd., at the Dorset Press,
Dorchester, Dorset

The publisher's policy is to use paper manufactured from sustainable forests.

About the Author

Jonathan Herring is a Fellow in Law at Exeter College, Oxford University. He has written many learned tomes on Family Law; Medical Law and Criminal Law. When not teaching or writing he enjoys laughing, hammocks, and depressing French films.

ACKNOWLEDGEMENTS

I am very grateful to my wife, Kirsten Johnson, for all her help in writing this book and for not tickling me too much. My three children, Laurel, Jo and Darcy, provide endless laughter and joy for which I am for-ever grateful. Many thanks too to the team at Pearson who have been hugely supportive and full of excellent ideas, especially Elie Williams and Laura Blake.

CONTENTS

ABOUT THE AUTHOR   vii

ACKNOWLEDGEMENTS   ix

INTRODUCTION   xiii

1 THE WOMAN WHO TICKLED TOO MUCH   1

2 THE GOLD-DIGGER WHO FOUND NO GOLD   19

3 SLAVES AND COHABITANTS   39

4 THE WAGs DIVORCE   53

5 THE SECRET IN THE SOCK DRAWER   65

6 THE MIX-UP AT THE IVF CLINIC   81

7 BEYOND THE CALL OF DUTY?   93

8 THE MIRACLE BABY   105

9 DEVOTED FATHERS   121

10 DIVORCING YOUR PARENTS   135

11 THINGS PARENTS DISAGREE ON   147

12 A TRAGIC CONVICTION   165

13 WHAT'S IN A NAME?   179

14 WHICH OF THEM DID IT?   191

15 TO THE CARE HOME   205

INTRODUCTION

ALL FAMILIES ARE DIFFERENT. I write as the father of three young children, as a son, a stepson, a brother, a stepbrother, a cousin to a host of people, and the husband of a wife who is not always the easiest person to live with. Then again, neither am I. Families are not easy. They are complicated, challenging and unpredictable. But they are also rewarding, inspiring and can be great fun. They are the glue that holds society together.

In surveys people consistently list their family as the most important thing in their lives. More important than work or wealth. Yet few of us stop to think about what our families are, or how they work. It used to be a father, a mother and 2.2 children. But this is the twenty-first century and we've moved on a bit.

Now British law finally allows a same-sex couple to declare: 'We are Family' and science has made it possible for them to have children. Ideas of what makes a good parent are constantly being challenged. What are fathers for these days? And what of mothers? Is the 'working mother' a necessity, an evil or a role model?

What about older people? Who is going to care for them and how are we going to afford the care of our ageing population?

Each of you reading this book will have your own unique family situation and attitudes as to what constitutes a family. To some, cats, dogs and teddy bears play a more important role in family life than grumpy great aunts.

And nowhere are the intricacies of family life more exposed than in a court of law. Every foible, fallacy and failing is laid bare in front of the judiciary. And some of the mishaps people get themselves into are pretty mind-boggling.

As an outsider looking in the law can seem an inscrutable beast. Most people, when gazing up at the Royal Courts of Justice in London, are likely to feel intimidated. It is an imposing Victorian gothic building, made all the more impressive by the seemingly endless tide of bewigged barristers leading their bewildered clients through its enormous doors. Inside it is cavernous and, unconsciously, all conversations are whispered. And it's here that decisions are made which will have profound consequences. People leaving these court rooms may have had their lives changed for ever.

But, family law can also be quite entertaining, as I think some of the cases you are about to read prove. I have chosen cases which will amuse, intrigue, beguile and fascinate you. Sometimes they will make you sad or irritated, but I hope that they will also make you pause to think about how you might react if you were faced with the same dilemmas.

There is of course the woman who tickled too much (can one really have too much tickling?); and the couple who had trouble conceiving, so asked the usher from their wedding *and* two other friends to help them out (yes, the wife was really game to try it the natural way). Then there are the naturists; the sado-masochists; the gold-diggers; those so desperate for children they could believe in miracles; the list goes on ... . Some of these cases attracted considerable media attention; others were more quietly reported only in the official law reports. All of them raise issues of huge importance to our society and they all affect us and the way we run our family lives.

So I hope you will become just as fascinated as I am about Family Law when you've read about these cases. And if some of them do bring you to tears, or make you want to tear your hair out, or even throw this book across the room that's fine; this is not a book to be read passively, but one to savour and mull over.

As for me, family life is never boring. Yes, it is complicated. It involves give and take and compromise. And it involves letting my wife rewrite this introduction, as she has just done. But we (and this introduction) are all the better because of it. Families mould us, make us, change us and fulfil us. So embrace yours, whatever it is, and enjoy it.

Jonathan Herring
Oxford, 2009

1

THE WOMAN WHO TICKLED TOO MUCH

WHEN SHOULD A HUSBAND or wife be able to divorce their spouse? Many people think these days that once one party wishes to end the marriage there is no point keeping the marriage alive. The law may as well allow a divorce. However, few people would be keen to see the kind of 'drive through' divorce system that some states in the United States have. The current law requires parties to make an allegation of adultery or unreasonable behaviour unless the couple are willing to separate for two years before getting a divorce. Few couples seem willing to do that. That means the courts are still required to deal with cases where one spouse has behaved in a sufficiently bad way to justify a divorce being granted. Over the years, there has been a wide range of unusual behaviour which has been cited in divorce petitions.

One particularly unusual divorce case was heard in several courts and only finally resolved on 16 July 1963. It involved a divorce application made by a wife on the basis of her husband's cruelty. The couple had lived together for only six months, but by then the wife had already had enough. At the heart of her complaint was her husband's persistent demands that she tickle the soles of his feet, the top of his head, or his back.

It all started just a week into the marriage when the husband returned home from work, removed his shoes and socks and demanded that his wife tickle his feet. The wife reported that she found the request 'peculiar' and refused. The husband threatened not to talk to her unless she did as he asked. For some wives that might not be so much a threat as a blessing. Not so for Mrs Lines. She complied with his request. But that seemed to stoke his appetite for tickling rather than quenching it. Nearly every night from then on he insisted on being tickled. Mrs Lines complained to the court that he *even* demanded this when they were watching television. That, one can imagine, was just beyond the pale. Some nights the tickling sessions went on for over four hours. The reports suggest that although Mrs Lines would have enjoyed being tickled, Mr Lines never reciprocated.

The tickling got too much for the wife and in January 1959 she left the husband for two days. She only agreed to return when the husband promised to give up tickling. But, as many wives will attest, it is as difficult to get a husband to change his habits as it is persuade a cat to give up napping. Although Mr Lines promised to give it up for good, within a few days he was importuning for tickling.

By February 1959 things were in a dire state. The wife went to see her doctor who reported her to be suffering from acute anxiety and stated that the excessive tickling meant that she was no longer able to keep her hands still. This tickling had clearly ceased to be a laughing matter. The problems with her hands persisted. Indeed when she gave evidence before the court the judge noticed that Mrs Lines' hands moved in what appeared to be involuntary tickling movements.

The husband had been warned of the effects of his tickling demands on his wife's health and yet had insisted on it with no regard to her well-being. That amounted to cruelty, on which grounds the divorce was granted.

We do not know whether Mr Lines' enthusiasm for foot tickling had erotic motivation. But if it did he would not be alone. Dr Benamou has written a lengthy academic analysis of the erotic possibilities of feet and shoes. He is the Honorary President and Editorial Director of the French Journal, *Foot Medicine and Surgery*. He reports that the Egyptian queen Hatshepsout had servants who would tickle her to great ecstasy with peacock feathers. He also refers to the case of a rich woman in New York who several times a week would rub her feet with dog food so that when her two Pomeranians came into her flat they would lick her feet. That was said to cause an 'erotic ecstasy'. Grand Duchess Anna Leopoldovana employed sex foot-ticklers for each foot. In the eighteenth century, when she lived, able foot-ticklers could demand high fees. Maybe Mrs Lines was born into the wrong century. Her evident skills could have made her a fortune!

The issue of foot tickling appears a common one. On the Yahoo! Answers website, one questioner asked, 'My wife loves having her feet tickled, does anyone else think that is weird?' Of the twenty-one people who replied, not a single one thought it odd at all. Several wrote in with other suggestions for toe stimulation. Indeed there are suggestions on that website for what instruments could be used to tickle feet. This includes: 'Feathers, pinwheels (think of pizza cutters, but smaller, and not to be painful with, just to tickle), fingers, hair, a silky scarf.'

Elsewhere on the web a rather different tickling problem has been posed:

My husband, since we have been dating has excessively tickled me. I am so sensitive that I once fell off a chair and caused a whole scene. He does not stop when I ask him. My sister did the same thing when I was little and she called it tickle torture. She would tickle me until I peed my pants. It is so frustrating. When my kids ask them to stop tickling, I get really upset and defend my children, just because I know how not fun it is.

It is not clear to what extent this form of tickle torture takes place, or whether it is a major course of marital stress.

If Mr Lines is still alive (he has somewhat sunk into obscurity) he might be drawn to a piece of research that a scientist is undertaking. He is seeking volunteers and asks:

Have you ever wondered why your feet are so ticklish? I've been doing research on laughter and ticklishness for years. I've already found some statistically significant facts about ticklishness that may surprise you. I'm still looking for volunteers to have their feet tickled. You can be of any ticklish level for the research.

He is not the only scientist interested in tickling. A group from the University of California explain that from their research they have discovered that tickling is an 'involuntary defence mechanism' that has developed through evolution. It is used to alert the brain to the fact that vulnerable parts of the body are being attacked. They suggest it is useful to distinguish two kinds of tickling: Garaglesis and Knismesis. The former is 'laughter associated tickling' and is a reflex reaction caused by heavy stroking of the skin. The latter, however, is caused by feather light movement across the skin which sends messages to the somatosensory cortexes of the brain. The team of scientists are still attempting to work out quite how the complex chemical and biological reactions that result from these different kinds of tickling cause their effects.

Mr and Mrs Lines with their feet tickling problems are not the only couple who had to have their marriage examined in painful detail by the courts. Nowadays it is rare for a divorce to be defended and so most petitions do not have to be heard in court. However, in the past, even if both couples wanted a divorce the matter had to be heard in public. The following are some of the more bizarre cases that came to court.

Mr and Mrs Le Brocq married in 1938, but in 1955 sought a divorce. The relationship had completely broken down. Mrs Le Brocq was described as having a domineering temperament. One of the judges described her as volatile and lively. He explained that she 'likes a certain kind of row occasionally' ('as many married people do' the judge added!). Mr Le Brocq was described as having an inferiority complex. He was said to be silent and morose. One judge described him as a man who withdraws into his shell. As you can imagine this produced a personality clash. The wife was fed up that her husband was not willing to have a row with her. Whenever she got angry he just shrugged his shoulders and left the room. The wife became completely exasperated with him. Indeed she developed an ulcer worrying about the situation. She excluded him from the bedroom and bolted the door, although he never again tried to enter it. The divorce was denied by the Court of Appeal. Although Mr Le Brocq's conduct was such that his wife could not be expected to put up with it, it could not be said to be cruelty. For about ten years they had lived in the same house, but separately. He said nothing but 'thank you' to the wife for days on end. That it was thought fit that they had to remain married is extraordinary. It is highly unlikely a court would take the same approach today.

Mr and Mrs Squire's marriage was also a sad one. The year is 1945. For four years Mr Squire had to put up with some very difficult behaviour from the wife. Whenever he started to fall asleep the wife would, for nights on end, keep him awake. She would demand that he read to her or talk to her. If he refused, she insisted that he performed menial tasks for her. This might include stripping the clothes from the bed; moving furniture round the room; switching lights on or off. By the end of the four years the husband was exhausted from severe sleep deprivation and his health was suffering. He was allowed a divorce on the basis that the wife's behaviour was cruel, even though it was not malicious. She had, Lord Justice Evershed explained, 'deprived him, time and time again, of the sleep which is no less necessary than food for bodily refreshment'. The wife suggested that he could have done more to get sleep. Lord Evershed commented: 'He might have retaliated with violence, or done so to a greater extent than he did, for it was proved that on some occasions he did strike her. The choice is not one likely to commend itself to a husband with a sense of duty and propriety or to a husband who loved his wife.' The comment gives a chilling insight into what was acceptable matrimonial behaviour in the late 1940s. The judge, fortunately, concluded that a divorce was appropriate in the Squires' case.

Mr and Mrs Richmond's relationship ended in more colourful circumstances. The case warns of the dangers of caravan holidays. Mr and Mrs Richmond decided one year to go on holiday with another couple, the Burfitts. During the holiday Mrs Richmond had sex with Mr Burfitt. It is not made explicit whether or not Mrs Richmond had proposed a holiday with the Burfitts precisely so this could be facilitated. But that may be so. Nevertheless, their activities left their spouses, Mrs Burfitt and Mr Richmond, together for long periods of time and they also found themselves attracted to each other. In due course Mrs Burfitt had sex with Mr Richmond. Lord Merriman, the then President of the Family division, described this in rather startling terms:

> " *It is common ground that in August 1950, this husband and wife went with another couple, named Burfitt, for a caravan holiday together with the three daughters of the Burfitts and another child and that in that atmosphere, with those young people about, on at least two occasions, by mutual consent these spouses agreed to an exchange of partners.* "

Quite why the presence of children created an atmosphere of 'wife swapping' is something of a mystery. Nevertheless, the crucial point for the court was that adultery was regarded as consented to by the respective parties. In other words Mr Richmond could not complain about Mrs Richmond's adultery, given his approval, or at least acceptance, of the practice.

11

On returning from the holiday Mrs Richmond and Mr Burfitt decided that they had been doing wrong and refrained from all sexual activity together. Mrs Burfitt and Mr Richmond were not, however, so stricken by conscience. They continued their relationship and indeed a child was born to Mrs Burfitt which Mr Richmond agreed was his. Eventually Mr Richmond moved in with Mrs Burfitt. No divorce the court ordered: Mrs Richmond was taken to have condoned the adultery. Not for the first time – or last time – in history, a wife came to regret going on a caravan holiday.

Mr and Mrs O'Neill could have done with *DIY SOS*, the television programme that seeks to repair the damage done by botched DIY jobs. Unfortunately that programme was not available back in 1975, although the divorce courts were. The couple had bought a flat after eighteen years of marriage and the husband started an extensive and prolonged period of renovation after they moved in. The primary problem, apparently, was dampness. The Court of Appeal noted, evidently with some opprobrium, that the husband did not seek advice on how to do the work. He raised the floorboards and filled the garden with rubble. A cement mixer was placed in the living room. The lavatory door was removed and it took over eight months for it to be replaced. Further, for some reason, the husband removed the curtains in the flat and these were also not replaced.

The Court of Appeal displayed their evident sympathies with the difficulties facing the wife:

" *He proceeded himself to do it in what must be supposed he thought was the best way of doing it in the circumstances; but he was not an expert in these matters, and he certainly was not by training a builder's labourer, and it was the work of a builder's labourer which to a large extent he was doing, carting out bucket by bucket this rubble from underneath the floorboards and depositing it outside. As a result, the flat was in such a condition during most of the time that the family were living there that it was an embarrassment to have visitors brought to it; and there was a particular embarrassment not only to visitors but for the wife and her daughter of the lavatory door being off.* "

But Mr O'Neill's inadequacies in the DIY department were not the end of his wife's complaints. Not at all. She also objected that he failed to keep himself clean. The wife said he hardly ever bathed himself and was a dirty man. Mr O'Neill vehemently denied this and explained that he washed once a week. It is perhaps rather surprising that the judge who first heard the case concluded that the husband was a clean man. He denied the divorce.

The Court of Appeal, however, granted the divorce. They criticised the first judge who had read from the Prayer Book that a spouse was required to take the other 'for better or for worse'. They maintained that the law was less strict. If a husband behaved unreasonably a divorce was available. In this case Mr O'Neill had done so. Divorce granted.

A final example of an unhappy marriage has not yet hit the courts, but it seems destined to do so. Amy Pollard, in the summer of 2008, discovered her husband was committing adultery. This was the second time she had caught him at it. But this was not your normal kind of adultery. He had been using his animated character on Second Life to have sex with a female character, on Second Life. The first time she had found out about his virtual affair was when she found his character having sex with an online call girl. She had woken suddenly from a nap only to find her husband on the computer, with his character 'at it' with another character. She later amplified what 'at it' meant: 'I caught him cuddling a woman on a sofa in the game. It looked really affectionate.' She had hired an online private detective to investigate him. The online detective set a 'honey trap' for the husband in Second Life and he had fallen for it, hook line and sinker. His marriage came unstuck.

You might think the wife was over-reacting. However, the couple actually met in virtual reality. Her alter ego (Laura Skye) and his (Dave Barmy) met on Second Life and got on well. They decided to meet in real life and soon moved in together and got married twice ... naturally enough in St Austell and then on Second Life! The Second Life wedding was modelled on David and Victoria Beckham's marriage, complete with carriage and castle.

The solicitor dealing with the case said she was not at all surprised by the circumstances of the marriage breakdown. This was her second divorce case involving Second Life that week, she told the press. Amy Pollard's husband is now engaged to the woman he was having a virtual affair with on Second Life. Amy herself had met a new partner, predictably on an online game, but this time, World of Warcraft.

And what is the future for the law of divorce? Well, here's a prediction: it will become much more commercialised. In 2008 a 'divorce fair' was held in Vienna. Men were allowed to come on the Saturday and women on the Sunday. There were a wide range of specialist services available for divorcing couples. They were offered everything from 'life crisis experts' to DNA testing laboratories. From estate agents to travel agents offering therapeutic holidays tailored to a person seeking to recover from divorce. Brighton followed suit with a divorce fair in March 2009. Over 300 people attended despite complaints that the event was seeking to make money from people's misery. Making money from divorce is, of course, nothing new. Lawyers have been at it for years.

2

THE GOLD-DIGGER WHO FOUND NO GOLD

JULIA ORISKA LAMBE CLARK was described by the judge of the Court of Appeal as 'a woman of considerable charm and physical attraction'. That a modern-day judge would say such a thing about a party to a case might be thought surprising. But that tells you a lot about Julia Clark. She was the kind of woman who caused men of a certain age to set aside their normal scruples.

Julia Oriska was born on 7 November 1949, in Southampton. She met George Clark for the first time at a Christmas party hosted by her former mother-in-law on 22 December 1991. Before the party, Julia Clark's long-term financial future looked bleak. Her house had been mortgaged up to the hilt and her liabilities exceeded her assets. Unfortunately she suffered from several phobias which meant she was unable to work. In short her financial position was desperate. Not so for Mr Clark. He had over £1 million on deposit at the bank and a further

£2 million on the stock exchange. Not only were their financial situations somewhat disparate, so too were their ages. At the infamous Christmas party, Mr Clark was a sprightly seventy-seven, while Ms Clark was a touch over forty.

Perhaps, given such facts, their meeting at the party could have had but one eventuality. He fell in love with her; and she with his money. Fortuitously, from Julia Clark's point of view, the relationship developed quickly and by February 1992 Mr Clark had purchased a house for her which he redeveloped at a cost of £250,000. By 7 April the wedding day had arrived. Their wedding was a modest affair at the Haringey register office, with only three guests. According to one press report Julia Clark wore a miniskirt, four-inch heels and three-inch nails. The outfit was finished off with a pekingese under her arm.

Unfortunately, the wedding day did not continue as one imagines Mr Clark hoped it would. Julia left him at the reception. There was to be no consummation of the marriage that night. Nor indeed would there ever be. This dire start to matrimonial bliss was reflected by the fact Mr Clark applied to have the marriage annulled just two months after the wedding day. However, it seems there was some kind of reconciliation because the petition was dismissed by consent.

The reconciliation was short-lived and it did not lead to cohabitation or consummation. Julia Clark later told a journalist that it was never imagined that their marriage would have a physical side. Indeed, she intimated, her husband would not have been capable of consummating the union. Rather than engaging in sex, Mr Clark engaged in heavy expenditure. He paid off the remaining £146,000 mortgage on Julia's home. Then, in what may have been an attempt to buy the appropriate love nest in which consummation could take place, he bought three London flats. None of this worked. They lived apart. Mr Clark visited his wife on several weekends. But these visits never led to consummation; indeed it appears there was only one occasion on which she even admitted him to her bedroom.

Things got worse. Julia Clark refused to acknowledge to friends that she was married to George Clark, apparently due to the embarrassment she felt at being married to a much older man. She forced him to move into a caravan in the garden. And she seemed to be able to manipulate Mr Clark into any expenditure she wished. He spent over £100,000 on renovation of Julia's boat, although in its improved state it was only worth £35,000. Another property named Wellow Park was purchased which cost nearly £750,000. This was the former home of Florence

Nightingale. Having purchased this property the wife arranged for the home to be divided into two halves, one for him and one for her. By now you will be unsurprised to learn that they were not of equal size. His was said to be 'small, dark and depressing', while hers was rather grand. The judge hearing the case stated: 'It is clear to me that the wife's constant demands and her vituperative behaviour if she did not get her own way were wearing the husband down.'

Divorce proceedings were instituted by the husband, but again they were ended by consent after Julia agreed to live together with George in the main part of Wellow Park. The court found that, despite what had happened, the husband still loved his wife. His gifts continued to flow and the London flats and Wellow Park were transferred into his wife's name. Most ironic of all, the wife persuaded the husband to buy her a racehorse with the name 'Lucky Lover'. A less apt name it is hard to imagine. None of this improved their relationship and there was still no consummation or indeed much companionship. The judge found that, by this point, the husband had become a 'sad and sorry' figure.

His humiliation was not quite complete. Using money originating from her husband Julia Clark purchased an ice-cream shop and installed a man fifteen years younger than herself as the manager. Inevitably, given that age disparity was not one of Julia's hang-ups they became lovers and she moved him into Wellow Park. As well as running the ice-cream shop, he tried his hand at acting, having walk-on roles in the television series *Casualty* and *Dangerfield*. He subsequently told the press he had not caused her marriage to end and indeed had got on well with Mr Clark. This man, John Lanasis, later spoke to the press. He stated, 'I am not Mrs Clark's lover. A woman who is seventy-five percent disabled by agoraphobia would not be able to cope physically or mentally with a lover.' He repeated his denials that he was Julia Clark's lover, adding that 'lover is a dirty word'. He preferred to say they were just friends.

Mr Clark's position by Easter 1997 was grim. Julia had taken away his telephone and, worse still, his buzzer. The buzzer enabled him to enter or leave the front gate of Wellow Park. He was, effectively, a prisoner in the small part of the house his wife allowed him to reside. His wife was consistently belittling and humiliating him. Most of his money had gone and he had lost contact with almost all of his friends. Mr Clark's state of despair was manifested by a suicide attempt on 20 May 1997. He took an overdose of sleeping pills. Following this he was moved to a private nursing home. Even then he decided to leave the nursing home and return to his wife. But not for long; on

5 September with the help of the police he was removed. Proceedings for divorce were soon filed. His ordeal was coming to an end.

Mr Clark's solicitors made an offer to settle the case by paying Julia effectively £592,500. An offer rightly regarded as generous. True to form, she rejected it. Further negotiations, it seemed, had little chance of success and, indeed, the case went to trial and was heard by Mr Harward–Smith QC who was sitting as a deputy judge.

The issue for the judge was how to divide the couple's assets. At the date of the hearing Mr Clark's assets were about £3.2 million gross, while the wife had £1.2 million. Mrs Clark's case was that she was a caring wife and an astute businesswoman. She portrayed her husband as senile and difficult. She had, despite his problems, cared for him and his financial affairs. Indeed, she claimed that the husband, as a result of her care, was £1 million better off. The husband's case was that the wife was wicked and he had lost £1 million during their marriage. As is often true in family law cases, it was hard to believe that the parties before the court were talking about the same marriage.

A key moment during the trial came when Mr Clark offered his wife £453,500 (less than his earlier offer due to the spiralling legal costs). This too was rejected. The judge was going to have to produce a judgment to resolve this case. In his judgment, Mr Harward-Smith QC, found the husband's version of events to be the more accurate.

Then Mr Harward-Smith turned to the application of the law. On divorce, all the assets that a couple have can be redistributed by the courts. The courts are given a broad discretion. The factors that they should consider are listed in the Matrimonial Causes Act 1973, but they are simply things to take into account. Judges are left to determine what distribution of the property would be fair in all the circumstances. In fact, for most couples the court will not be particularly interested in who owns what property. In most cases what is far more important is what the needs of the parties are. Apart from wealthy couples, the harsh reality in modern times is that both spouses are going to be significantly worse off after a divorce than they were before. The courts often struggle to ensure that the basic needs of both of the parties and any children are met. For wealthier couples there is usually enough to ensure that the essential needs of the parties are met. In which case the courts tend to divide the assets the couple have accumulated during the marriage equally between them, unless there is a particularly good reason not to.

In the Clarks' case, the judge awarded the wife assets and cash totalling £552,500, a package which would cost the husband £827,000, because he would be responsible for the legal costs in the case. At first sight this is an astonishingly large sum. Especially in light of the judge's comments made in his judgment, about the wife's behaviour during the marriage. He noted that the marriage was short, and indeed was 'never a proper marriage'. The wife had married for the money. He found that the wife's financial contribution to the marriage was negative, causing a loss to the husband of not far short of £1 million. He stressed that her behaviour had led Mr Clark to attempt suicide. So how could the judge justify the award?

Well, Mr Hayward-Smith QC emphasised that Mrs Clark had nearly £200,000 in debts. He also placed great weight on the fact that Mr Clark had said that he wanted to be generous to his wife and had shown that with his earlier settlement offers. The award to the wife of just over half a million pounds would be just sufficient to pay off her debts, purchase a modest home and provide a basic level of income. The judge concluded that this is what the husband 'in his heart of hearts' wanted.

Before you despair of the judiciary and take to marching on the streets to protest at the incompetence of judges, the story is not yet over. Both the husband and the wife appealed. Of course Mr Clark was seeking to have the award reduced, while Mrs Clark demanded an increase. The case was heard in the Court of Appeal. One of England's leading family law judges, Lord Justice Thorpe, gave the judgment.

At the centre of the wife's case was evidence that she suffered from agoraphobia and had an over-whelming psychological need to remain at Wellow Park. She produced evidence from experts who testi-fied that there was a significant risk she would commit suicide if she was obliged to leave her house. She had had to be brought to the Appeal Court by ambulance and was attended by paramedics during the hearing. Further, Mrs Clark was currently living at Wellow Park with a duck known affectionately as Dynamo Duck, a horse, donkeys, pigs, goats, cats, chicken, geese and peacocks. She could not keep all these animals if she were required to leave.

Mrs Clark was represented by her son from her previous marriage, Mr Doveton, a final year history and politics student at Southampton University. He was not legally qualified, but she was unable to afford legal representation. Mr Doveton was given special permission by the court to represent her. He sought to challenge the findings of fact by the judge, deny-ing that his mother had been cruel. However, in cases where there is an appeal, it is rare for the Court of

Appeal to depart from the findings of fact made by the trial judge. Not least because the trial judge, unlike the Court of Appeal, had the opportunity to hear all of the witnesses. The Court of Appeal makes its decisions based on written evidence.

The husband had a senior barrister, Mr Timothy Scott QC, presenting his case. The husband's appeal centred on two points in particular. The first, predictably, was that the wife's conduct had not sufficiently been taken into account. The second was that the wish of the husband to be generous should not have been given weight.

Lord Justice Thorpe started by considering the wife's appeal. He was rather blunt and described it as hopeless. The first judge had considered the wife's illness and the possible impact of requiring her to move from Wellow Park. He had preferred the evidence of the experts who did not think there was a high risk of suicide. Lord Justice Thorpe thought there was no reason to depart from the first judge's conclusion.

As to the husband's appeal Lord Justice Thorpe was far more sympathetic, particularly as regards Mrs Clark's conduct. The key statutory provision is section 25(2)(g) of the Matrimonial Causes Act 1973 which requires the court to take into account the conduct of the parties if it is such that it is 'inequitable to disregard'. Lord Justice Thorpe thought the conduct of the wife in this case matched this description well. In fact, he thought it would be hard to 'conceive graver marital misconduct'. It was 'as baleful as any to be found in the family law reports'. Indeed, he suggested that had the trial judge decided to award the wife nothing, that would have been a permissible order. However, it was not the order he was minded to make. Lord Justice Thorpe's hands were somewhat tied in that sums had already been paid to the wife. He thought ordering the wife to return cash would simply lead to further delays and litigation. Lord Justice Thorpe settled on the wife being awarded a total of £175,000, which had been the husband's proposed sum presented to the Court of Appeal.

As a result of the Court of Appeal's judgment Julia Clark was far worse off than she would have been if she had accepted her husband's offer made early on in the negotiations. Indeed 6 May 1999, the day of the Court of Appeal's decision, was doubly not a good day for Julia Clark. She had been standing as a Labour Party candidate in the election for Test Valley Council. The results of the election came just hours after the Court of Appeal judgment. She fared no better with the voters than she had with the judiciary. She came a distant third, polling just 89 votes.

Following the case *The Times* reports her to have said:

> People are saying I am a poor little rich girl. They
> should see the inside of the house – I don't have a
> shower and there's electric cable lying around. ...
> Where else do I go? I've got all my animals. I can't
> be separated from them. I've only got one son and
> my animals are like my extended family.

Not surprisingly, Mrs Clark did not leave her home
quietly. She left only after the Deputy Under-Sheriff
of Hampshire had issued a warrant to take possession
of the house. Her menagerie of pets were allowed to
stay there until a new home could be found. In a final
bid to prevent repossession she had taken two Koso-
var refugees to live in the house's grounds. They too
were required to leave.

Mrs Clark was true to style and left Wellow Park
in her Bentley. According to reporters she departed
in tears. As she left, her partner John Lanasis, 34,
said, 'She is distraught. Mr Clark may have won the
battle but he has not won the war.'

Lord Justice Thorpe, who heard the case in Court
of Appeal, described this as 'one of the most extraordinary marital histories I have ever encountered'.
That is not surprising. The case, however, raises
some important and interesting issues.

Clearly, at the heart of this case was the bad conduct of the wife. But, is it really possible to decide

who is at fault in a divorce case and who is not? Is it always obvious? What is bad conduct in a marriage? Is a husband who spends a lot of time with his friends at the pub behaving badly? Is a wife whose laundry skills are below par to be deemed to have misbehaved? And even if we can agree on what is bad conduct, is it not often a case of six of one and half-a-dozen of the other? One Cambridge academic has even suggested that in a scenario where the husband has committed adultery, he might have been driven to it by the coolness of his wife. You might not want to go that far, but in many cases neither party will be blameless.

Even in the case of the Clarks, the question of bad conduct is not without doubt. The experienced journalist Decca Aitkenhead met Julia Clark after the divorce and found her to be a complicated character. She describes her as removed from reality and 'shrinking into herself, covering her face and twisting her shoulders as if she were crying'. Indeed her increasingly bizarre behaviour suggests not a calculating gold-digger, but a rather sad, lonely and confused person. Much of her childhood and twenties was taken up with caring for her elderly father. And, although the court were rightly critical of the wife, was the husband not to blame too? To one journalist Julia Clark stated, 'I think he wanted a trophy wife he could show off to friends, but when he realised I wasn't well enough to go to functions with him he got quite cross, because I wasn't the filly he thought I was.' This paints a different picture of the relationship. If she was just after his money, perhaps he was just wanting to buy a trophy wife. Mr Clark was willing to use his money to gain the hand of a much younger woman. Neither of them should come out of this divorce with much credit.

Further was not the criticism of the wife here overblown? The judges in this case said this was some of the worse marital misconduct they had ever heard about, but was what Mrs Clark did really worse than the violence and abuse that women and children suffer at the hands of their husbands/fathers, examples of which routinely come before family judges?

You may not be persuaded by the general argument that you should not take conduct into account because it is usually very difficult to know who is to blame when a marriage has broken down. That may be true in some, perhaps many, cases. But that does not mean that where it is clear that one party has behaved badly the court should disregard it. Even so, you must consider the time and effort that it will take a court to make a proper assessment to determine who has behaved badly.

You may still be unconvinced, and think that surely there are some cases where the court can determine that one party is clearly proved to be at fault, without it taking too long to determine. But is it the role of the courts to attach blame for conduct which is immoral? Certainly where people commit crimes, they are rightly punished in the criminal courts. But, it is not normally the role of the courts to punish people for conduct which is merely immoral. In one case the Court of Appeal criticised a husband who had committed adultery and used it to justify requiring him to pay a hefty sum in a divorce settlement. The House of Lords rejected the Court of Appeal's approach, in that case saying only the most severe forms of conduct should be taken into account. One academic writing on the Court of Appeal's decision (rather bravely) suggested that the judiciary should not condemn people for committing adultery, and should not punish them by making financial orders on divorce, unless they could be sure there were none among their own number who had committed adultery! Once judges take up the role of deciding who is behaving immorally or not they enter tricky water. Should it not be left to the family and friends of the couple to heap blame as appropriate? The punishment of sinners is not, perhaps, for human judges.

There can, then, be a strong case for saying that conduct should not be considered by the courts. The courts should focus on the needs of the parties and the assets they have, and seek to distribute those in a fair way. Using bad behaviour as a reason for increasing or reducing an award is far more problematic than at first appears.

What happened next to Mr and Mrs Clark is largely unknown. Julia Clark turned to writing books for children and George Clark moved to Scotland to live with relatives. The case is perhaps a lesson for us all. Mr Clark hoped to buy glamour, youth and excitement. It went badly wrong. He ended up unhappy and suicidal. Mrs Clark saw in her elderly husband a way out of her financial worries. I doubt she ended up any happier as a result of the marriage.

Perhaps the one person left smiling (apart from the lawyers) was a Mr Charles Marshall, who (shortly before the marriage we have been discussing), was in his late seventies and a millionaire. He met a Julia Clark at the Romsey Agricultural Show. Within a couple of weeks she had moved into his farmhouse, and was 'always walking about with nothing on'; talking of marriage. He was later to comment:

> She was after getting married, but it's ridiculous to marry a man of my age when you're her age. She always wore revealing clothes and had her boobs hanging out. And she'd come and sit on the arm of

my chair with her skirt round her waist ... Sex-wise, it didn't interest me because there was nothing I could do about it. I'm too old.

He wisely ordered her to leave his house. An insightful old man. And a rather relieved one.

3

SLAVES AND COHABITANTS

MISCHON DE REYA ARE ONE of the most respected law firms in the world. Their family department has dealt with many high profile cases, not least Princess Diana's divorce settlement from Prince Charles. Their website assures readers: 'Our team specialises in assisting UK and international high net worth and high profile individuals. We resolve issues with discretion and sensitivity - ensuring that your interests and those of your family come first.' Yet when Mr Sutton and Mr Staal walked through their doors seeking advice, the company became embroiled in a most bizarre case.

Mr Sutton and Mr Staal met through an advertisement in *Gay Times*. Mr Staal was a wealthy Swedish businessman. Mr Sutton worked as an air steward, appropriately enough, for Virgin Atlantic. He supplemented his income by working as a male prostitute. Mr Staal contacted Mr Sutton, expressing an interest in using Mr Sutton's skills. They soon met. Mr Justice Hart in his judgment in the case noted that 'It is evident that Mr Staal found the particular services offered by [Mr Sutton] peculiarly gratifying.' Their relationship was based on Mr Sutton acting as a master and Mr Staal being the slave. Cupid's arrow seems to have hit its target with full force. Indeed their initial meeting went so well that Mr Staal suggested that the arrangement become a permanent one. He was willing to move to London to become Sutton's full-time slave. He offered to make Sutton heir to his fortune of over half a million pounds, and give Sutton all of his future income (some £6,000 per month). In return, he asked that Sutton treat him as a slave. He asked Sutton to 'keep me in a firm grip, taking away all my personal belongings, and leaving me totally to your mercy'. Staal encouraged the use of a whip or cane if he showed any disobedience.

Sutton's response to Staal's proposal might be thought to indicate that in his case Cupid's arrow was less on target. He suggested the creation of a Trust to govern their relationship. Property was to be bought in 'The Master's' name and £500,000 placed in a Luxembourg bank account that would become 'the Master's' when 'The Slave died'.

The couple signed a document they drafted themselves on 16 September 1997 which included the following terms (with Sutton being referred to as 'I' or 'me'):

'Statement of Trust

(1) I must promise to live with you in April 97.

(2) You must promise to live with me.

(3) You must promise to finance me with £3000/month starting 20th September, until 20th March.

(4) We must ensure everything is done legally.

(5) I trust you with my head, and now with my heart, and I will work towards ensuring that the relationship goes very well. For this to happen you must be prepared for me to become extremely angry, and extremely demanding. I am naturally demanding, however other slaves in the past have not been anywhere near my expectations – therefore you must work towards excellence at all times, and, whilst I promise to take care of you should you become sick or in old age, you must work with only one thing in your mind and that is: 'The well being and comfort of your MASTER'.

(6) You must promise to me, for this relationship to work, that you make it so that I have as much power over everything as is physically possible.

(7) The relationship will not work unless I have absolute power.

Agreement between Staal & Sutton

- As of April 1997 the above two named will reside in the same premises.

- The conditions of the cohabitation will be that Sutton is totally, totally in control.

- Staal will act only on instruction and command by Sutton, unless, Sutton asks the opinion of Staal.

- You will obey [i.e. Staal] everything I say, my well being is number one, yours is number two. I will keep you as I see fit, and I shall make all the decisions, you will have no authority in the household *at all*.

- Should you disobey or not reach Sutton's high standards you will be severely punished.

- Sutton will, at his discretion, lock you away.

- You will dress as I tell you, should we be in public you will never undermine my authority, you will act as my personal assistant if in a restaurant, or shop or other public place.

- You will not be allowed access to my quarters of the apartment should I instruct you leave them. You will not be allowed access to any outgoing telephone lines.

- You will be permitted an incoming telephone (with use of emergency service number only) and you will not know the number.

- I will ensure you are registered with BUPA private health insurance.

- You will be given around £300/month by me.

- In effect you are my property – I will essentially own you and will have ultimate power over you and all that you do.
YOU WILL NEVER TELL ME WHAT TO DO (unless I ask your advice).

- Only in totally, totally extreme situations will you be permitted to make suggestions – should you abuse this privilege you will be withdrawn the right to suggest anything.

- When you speak to me you will refer to me as SIR, you will only speak to me in humble manner and should NEVER use a condescending tone.

- I will never be expected to be available for you, if I want to go out alone or be alone you will stay in your quarters and will not move until I permit you to do so. I will keep all your identification, such as passport, driving licence.

- You will eat what I tell you, unless I give you permission to choose if out, or if I want you to cook for me.

- I will ensure you are registered at a health club and you will be permitted to use it at least four times per week, this will be your time for yourself.

- Each day you will have your duties, normally starting with bringing my breakfast and then continuing to serve throughout the day.

- You will be permitted, having firstly consulted with me, one to three outside contacts – with which you may communicate, having asked my permission to do so.'

Our devoted couple were understandably unsure of
the legal enforceability of their agreement and it
was at this point they entered the hallowed portals
of Mischon de Reya. There they met an assistant
solicitor, a Mr Perchal. They sought advice on
drafting a cohabitation agreement which would
govern their relationship. Mr Perchal said he was
willing to draft such an agreement although he
warned them the legal enforceability of such a contract would be questionable. He also advised the
couple that Mr Staal should receive independent
legal advice. That was commendable, because a
lawyer should not act for two clients whose interests
could conflict. Staal reassured Mr Perchal that he
would do so, although Staal, being a man of his
word, checked with his Master to ask if he could
have permission to see a solicitor.

Mr Perchal, acting in accordance with his clients'
instructions drafted a 'Deed of Cohabitation' for the
parties. The Deed lacked the colourful nature of the
agreement the parties had drafted together and was
in more formal legal language. Still, it made clear
that Staal was to give Sutton most of his property in
the event of the end of the relationship. The agreement was signed by the parties.

The signing of the deed, however, appeared to
precipitate a decline in their relationship. A few

weeks later Sutton received a letter from a firm of solicitors instructed by Staal, requiring the return of all gifts and payments and an acknowledgement that the cohabitation deed was void. The letter even added that the police may be contacted 'as we believe there may be criminal implications and we propose contacting *Gay Times* in which we understand you advertise'. There were threats of emergency injunctions. Staal's bank denied Sutton access to any credit facilities in connection with accounts opened by Staal. The Slave, it appeared, had turned.

But not for long. While his lawyers were busy writing such fearsome letters, Staal was writing to Sutton seeking a reconciliation. It was to no avail, and eventually it became clear there was no hope of these love birds being reunited.

One might have expected the case which ended up in court to have been between Mr Staal and Mr Sutton. But it did not follow that predictable route. Instead Sutton sued Mischon De Reya. He claimed that Mr Perchal had failed to give proper advice and had negligently drafted the cohabitation deed. As a result the cohabitation deed was void. The key question in the case soon became apparent: assuming the current deed was unenforceable, could Mr Perchal have drafted the deed in a way which would have been? If he could have done, but failed to do so, he could be found to have been negligent. If, however, he could not have done so, he could not be negligent.

Mr Justice Hart, decided in favour of Mischon de Reya and Mr Sutton left the court a poorer man. Perhaps wiser, too, because his case gave the learned judge the opportunity to provide Sutton with a thorough analysis of the law on cohabitation contracts. He started his discussion with a clear statement that, generally, cohabitation contracts are enforceable in English law if signed by unmarried couples. Not so pre-marriage or 'pre-nups'; but more on that shortly. Justice Hart accepted that in the past cohabitation contracts were regarded as contracts for immoral or 'meretricious' purpose and so were unenforceable. However, he explained, attitudes towards extra-marital sex had changed in recent years and that view would no longer be taken. In a rather sophisticated analysis Justice Hart thought the crucial distinction in the law was whether a contract was *between* couples who happened to be having sexual relations outside marriage; or whether it was a contract *for* sexual relations outside marriage. The first was perfectly valid, the second was not.

He thought this was a distinction which most people would readily understand. In a rather surprising turn of judicial phrase he thought that even 'a moron in a hurry' could see the contract in the

Sutton/Staal case was a contract for sexual services. Although much of the contract related to property matters, the judge, quoting from a barrister who likes long words, explained that the 'property relations "sprang from" the desire to give the sexual role-play verisimilitude'. In short, even the financial provisions in the contract were but a part of the sex game the parties were playing.

In any event, Mr Justice Hart concluded that even if the sexual services issue was ignored, the contract was almost bound to fall on the basis that Staal was acting under the undue influence of Sutton. The learned judge had read all of the relevant correspondence from Staal (which he wryly noted was 'voluminous'). This made it clear that 'the Slave' was entirely under his 'Master's' domination and not able to exercise his own will. So even if they had been able to draft the agreement in a way which was devoid of any sexual overtones, it would have been invalid because it was entered into under undue influence.

For lawyers the significance of this case lies in the clear statement that an unmarried couple can sign a cohabitation contract which will be enforceable, as long as they keep sex out of the contract. However, as mentioned earlier, married couples are treated differently: they cannot enter into binding 'pre-nups'. In many other countries a couple can sign these agreements and unless they can be shown to be legally invalid, they will be enforced. Not so in Britain. The reason the courts have given is that Parliament has bestowed upon the courts the job of deciding how property between spouses should be redistributed on divorce. A pre-marriage contract is an attempt by the parties to rob the courts of the responsibility Parliament has given to the judges.

This does not quite mean that the courts will place no weight on a pre-marriage contract. In one notorious case, Susan Crossley was divorcing for the fourth time. She was worth £18 million, largely from her previous marriages. Her first husband had been a member of the Kwik Save supermarket family. Her second was Peter Lilley, a tax exile. Husband number three was a pools heir and racing magnate. Her latest marriage only lasted fourteen months. She and her husband had signed a 'pre-nup' which, in essence, stated that they both were to keep their separate fortunes if their relationship was to fail. The judge held that he would give effect to the pre-nup unless the wife provided a very good reason why not to. The Court of Appeal held that this was a perfectly appropriate way for the judge to conduct the case. The couple were both wealthy and so there was no question of one of the parties ending up in dire poverty. Further, given their extensive experience of marriage and divorce, both parties could be taken to know exactly what they were doing. Indeed, they were independently advised before signing the agreement. Perhaps, most significantly, the court thought that it may well be that had the judge heard the case in full, he would have made the same order that was set out in the 'pre-nup'. So this case does not state that 'pre-nups' are now legally binding, just that they can be taken into account by the court in deciding what financial order to make.

It may well be that we are experiencing a shift in attitude towards 'pre-nups' in English law. In most other European countries they are legally binding. Maybe the law will change in England so that this will be true here too. Many people think that would be an admirable change in the law. After all, if a couple themselves have decided what would be a fair division of their property when they divorce, why should the judge claim to know any better? On the other hand, one may well wonder whether it is possible for a couple on the eve of their wedding to decide what would be a fair division of their assets in the event of a divorce many years into the future. Perhaps, most importantly, survey after survey has found that English couples do not like the idea of 'pre-nups': they are not very romantic, it is often said. And who said that romance was dead?

4

The WAGs Divorce

FOOTBALLERS' WIVES HAVE MADE a significant contribution to contemporary culture. They have been the subject of a popular television drama; caused the creation of a new word (WAGs – Wives And Girlfriends); and inspired a stereotype for a certain kind of attitude and behaviour. They have even been blamed for England's poor performance in the 2006 World Cup.

Perhaps, given the reputations of footballers and their wives, there have been surprisingly few divorces which have come before the courts. The most famous was Ray Parlour. He met his wife in February 1990. He was an apprentice footballer. She was employed by a local optician and was three years younger than him. She had left school aged sixteen with no GCSEs. He had recently signed a contract with Arsenal.

Ray Parlour played for Arsenal for fourteen years. He joined in 1989 as a trainee and made his debut against Liverpool in 1992. His earlier career was said to be marked with discipline issues. Most notably there was an incident involving a Hong Kong taxi driver when it was reported that Parlour tipped prawn crackers into the open bonnet of the taxi, leading to a punch-up and his subsequent arrest. However, his marriage and the arrival of Arsène Wenger as manager of Arsenal led to a rapid rise in his fortunes. He made twelve appearances for the England under-21 team. He became a regular player for Arsenal and was man of the match in the 1998 FA Cup final. In 1999 he made his debut for England. He won ten caps. Officially he did not score any goals, although in a match against Finland his shot crossed the line but was incorrectly declared not to be a goal by the linesman. He has been named the nineteenth greatest player in the history of Arsenal Football Club. Marc Overmars once called him the 'Romford Pele'. Whether that was intended as a compliment or not may be open to interpretation.

The Court of Appeal noted that Parlour's relationship with his future wife 'developed swiftly' and that they slept at his parents' home several nights a week soon after meeting. By 1994 Parlour encouraged his girlfriend to give up her employment as it was clear finances were not going to be an issue. Later that year they announced their engagement and in May 1995 moved into their first house together. The fact they relied on his parents' house as accommodation for so many years may be thought revealing. Five months after moving into the house, their first child was born. He was followed by two more children over the next four years. But in 2001, with their youngest child not yet two years old, the husband left home. He soon found another partner and had another child with her.

Lawyers tend to prefer it when couples negotiate their own settlement and there is no need to go to court. That way there is less work for the lawyer to do. The parties are normally content and the lawyer does not need to perform before a judge. Here the couple did well and reached agreement without too much difficulty: the wife was to keep the matrimonial home; a property in Norfolk; and £250,000. This amounted to some 37 per cent of the husband's assets. The dispute surrounded his future earnings, which for the next three years was estimated to be at over a million pounds a year. He had originally offered £120,000 per annum, an offer described by the judge as 'mean'.

When a court is deciding how to divide the assets on divorce it must determine what distribution of property would be fair. This involves considering a wide range of factors. Particularly relevant in this case was the fact that the marriage lasted just over three and a half years. However, the courts will look not just at the length of the marriage, but the length of the whole relationship, which in this case was for just over seven years. The court will also take into account the standard of living during the marriage. The *London Evening Standard* quoted a 'friend' of Karen Parlour as saying that her spending habits were 'more Romford than Bond Street'. Karen herself explained:

> As was to be the habit during our relationship, L [Mr Parlour] managed all our finances and I took little interest. My job was to run the home and to ensure all his needs were catered for. At no time during our relationship did I ask about what he earned. Money was never an issue between us throughout our relationship. He paid all the bills and gave me cash as and when I needed it.

Another factor the courts will consider is whether a spouse has suffered an economic loss due to the marriage. An obvious example would be where a wife gave up a career to undertake care of the children or general housekeeping duties. In that case the court will sometimes give the wife a sum of money to compensate her for her loss of earnings. However, in this case Karen Parlour had no established career before the marriage and there was no evidence that the marriage had harmed her earning potential.

Ray Parlour questioned his wife's contribution to the marriage. The judge held: 'There is no dispute, as I understand it, that the wife was a marvellous mother and ran the household efficiently and looked after the children and the husband to the very best of her considerable ability.' The husband, on the other hand, was the producer of a substantial income.

The husband argued that his future income should be seen as the product of his efforts. The wife could not claim a share in it. As his barrister put it: 'He is the one who performs the labour . ... He is the one who submits to Arsène Wenger's regime of behaviour and abstinence.' However, the court thought it wrong to see the income entirely due to the husband's efforts. It was noted by the judge:

66 *In the early days I am satisfied that the husband did participate in some of those drinking sessions. However the wife realised that that was the way to ruin and unhappiness and I am satisfied that in about the mid-1990s or slightly later she took a grip on the situation and encouraged and persuaded her husband to move away from that style of living. That rather bland description of what she did probably understates her contribution in this respect. In*

the mid-1990s the husband gave interviews to the press in which he publicly praised the wife for all that she did to bring him back from the brink. "

It is common for the courts to accept that a wife has supported a husband in his career through her home-making and child caring. Indeed the House of Lords have declared that the contribution to a marriage of a person who has spent their time looking after the house or children is equal to the person who contributes to the family in monetary terms. This means that in cases of wealthy couples the starting point is an equal division of assets. However, here the wife's claim is much stronger. But for her, it seems, her husband's career may have sunk without trace. She had a legitimate claim to make that without her contribution, his earnings would have been significantly less. The significance of her argument is that she could claim that not only the income during the marriage was in part a result of her efforts, but that his income in the future would be too.

But given that the husband was a footballer his high-earning career could not be expected to extend much beyond his mid-thirties. So in this case he was ordered to pay just under £450,000 per year for the next four years. However, the aim of this sum was not just to meet her ends but to enable her to put aside around £300,000 a year which could be used for investment to support her needs into the future. The Court of Appeal indicated that she could seek to have that period extended at the end of the fourth year if there was a good reason for doing so. Indeed in 2001 he moved to Middlesbrough and was reported to have taken a substantial wage cut. He later moved to Hull but no longer played for a league team after a season with them.

Ray Parlour joins the long list of celebrities who have been required to pay substantial sums of money in divorce settlements. Chris Tarrant was required to pay £12.5 million, half his fortune, on his divorce. The fourth Aga Khan had to pay £30 million on his divorce in 1995. Phil Collins was said to leave his wife with £17 million. Sir Paul McCartney left Heather Mills £24 million after their divorce, although she had sought much more.

Are payments of these kinds justifiable? Should a wife who has married a wealthy man (or indeed a husband who has married a wealthy wife) walk away after a few years of marriage with sums of money that most people would not earn with a lifetime of toil and labour? The critics of the current law could point to the fact that many wives of the rich and famous spend far less time and effort on child care or homemaking than do wives of less wealthy husbands.

Indeed the rich wives are likely to be supported by a small army of nannies and cleaners. So when the courts say they are acknowledging the importance of child care in making these awards, then it seems the money is going to the wrong people. Maybe a better argument is that the 'supporting spouse' has enabled the money earner to go out and create great wealth, by offering emotional, physical and domestic support. In other words, that the couple are seen as a partnership. They share the fruits of the domestic side of the relationship and should share the fruits of the money-earning side. The husband happily shares the fruits of the wife's labour, talents and skills; so the wife should have a share in his.

Another argument that has attracted some lawyers is that the wife has provided the husband with services during the marriage which he has not paid for: laundry, cleaning, cook, social PA, secretarial, sexual etc. Some people have attempted to calculate a monetary value on these services with different results being produced from between £30,000 and £400,000 a year. It could be argued that the wife should be paid in retrospect for these services if the relationship breaks up. Although whether paying the wife at the going rate for prostitutes for sex during marriage advances the feminist cause may be open to question! The value of the spouse could be increased if one includes the happiness caused by being married. One set of economists said that being married gives happiness of economic value of £120,000 per annum. In other words, you would need to spend £120,000 per year to get as much happiness as being married would give you. Mind you, I know a few spouses who would rather have the £120,000 per annum, than their spouse!

Perhaps at the end of the day the best response to claims that these wives don't deserve this much money is that no one does. It is absurd that their husbands have been earning so much. But it is no more unfair that the wives get a share of these ridiculous levels of wealth, than that their husbands do.

5

THE SECRET IN THE SOCK DRAWER

'TWENTY WAYS TO TELL if your husband is a man', ran a tabloid newspaper headline in 1997. Not, you might think, the most useful piece of public education. Anyway, do you need more than one way? What had inspired the story was the following extraordinary case.

On 17 July 1997 Ms J went through a ceremony of marriage with Michael. Nothing very unusual with that except that Michael had been born female. He had received some hormonal treatment and had a bilateral mastectomy. He lived as a man and did not tell Ms J that he had been born with female physical characteristics.

Michael was born in the north of England in a modest home. At birth he had the appearance of being a girl and was named Wendy. It seems, however, he was never happy with his sex and he dressed and acted as a boy. He got into trouble with the police when aged fourteen and gave his name as

Michael. From thenceforth he lived as Michael and no longer responded to the name Wendy. By the age of seventeen he was socially accepted as a male and at the age of twenty he began dating women. He had sex with them using what Lord Justice Ward described as 'an improvised prosthesis'. This, his lordship explained was a 'rigid device' which he wore 'more or less permanently'. He suffered depression at the age of twenty-six and explained that he felt trapped in a body that was not his. He was given counselling and a course of testosterone injections. These led to the growth of a beard and his voice breaking. He explained, 'I began to look like a man. At the same time my depression eased, and I felt a tremendous sense of relief.' At the time his doctor described him as having a case of 'true transsexualism'. This is perhaps best understood as a person having a strong sense of being a member of one sex, but having a body which matches the other sex. Michael's driving licence and National Insurance documents showed his new name, but his birth certificate could not be altered. It stated he had been born a woman. In December 1973 Michael underwent a bilateral mastectomy. Although the creation of a penis was recommended, he did not go through with that procedure. After the operation he started a new life in London and several years later he met the

plaintiff, Ms J (her name as given in the court proceedings, to avoid publicity).

Ms J had been brought up in circumstances which
were a stark contrast with Michael's more humble
origins. Lord Justice Ward described her background
as one of 'wealth and privilege'. She met the defendant when she was nineteen years old. She was
eleven years his junior and described as 'an unhappy
theology undergraduate disaffected with university'.
They met in the local pub where Michael was the
assistant manager and Ms J had a part-time job.

Not long after meeting they had sexual inter-
course, with the defendant using his false penis.
Significantly, the court emphasised that Ms J had no
real sexual experience prior to meeting Michael. It
seems that she did not think there was anything particularly amiss. Soon afterwards, they started living
together. On 7 July 1977 they went through a ceremony of marriage. During that ceremony the
defendant presented himself as a man and those
involved in the ceremony believed they were witness-
ing a marriage between a man and a woman.

According to Ms J the first inkling she had that all
was not as she thought occurred several years into
the marriage. She did something no wife should do.
She looked in her husband's sock drawer. There she
found the artificial penis. When she challenged her

husband about it he said he had used it as a sex aid with a former partner, but did not use it with her. She asked him to dispose of it. He said he would, but she later found it again under the mattress. It was at that point in the marriage she realised that he was using the artificial penis with her. But that did not cause her to question whether or not he was a man. Her assumption was that his penis was extremely small or deformed. Thereafter their sex life became more limited; indeed, it seems they had sex only twice a year.

In 1985 the couple sought fertility treatment from a fertility clinic. Donor sperm was used and a son was born in 1987 and a girl in 1992. Lord Justice Ward was later to state: 'The apparent ease with which they were able to obtain this treatment without the truth being disclosed or discovered is, for me, one of the puzzling and, I feel bound to add, unsatisfactory features of this case.' Before fertility treatment would be offered one would expect those involved to be satisfied the couple had fertility issues and efforts be made to ascertain the exact problem. It is worth noting that this couple was provided with the fertility treatment before the Human Fertilisation and Embryology Authority (HEFA) had been created. Since the HEFA's creation the whole area of assisted reproduction has become more tightly regulated.

By April 1994 the relationship had begun to break down. Ms J sought a divorce claiming that the husband had 'behaved in such a way that she could not be expected to live with him'. In May 1994 there was a serious argument between them. The defendant's manhood was the key issue. Michael undid his trousers and exposed his artificial penis. 'Is this not good enough for you?', he asked. To which her sad reply was: 'But it's not real'.

Shortly after that row Ms J confided in a friend that there were 'peculiarities about Michael's physique: his nipples, the scars under his arms, the fact that he used an artificial penis and the [blood stains] upon his underpants'. Her belief was that he was not well endowed, or even had a sexual deformity. What she did not realise was her friend was a part-time private detective and she soon went to work. Two days later she informed Ms J that the defendant had been born a girl. The very next day a copy of the birth certificate was produced in court. The judge at that hearing noted that when Ms J saw it she 'more or less collapsed'. She later started a course of counselling which continued for many months. She had been married for nearly seventeen years without realising her husband had been born a woman.

For Ms J the discovery that her husband was not a man came as an utter shock and destroyed the marriage.

It seems Michael found it difficult to understand why it all mattered so much. As he was later to write: 'I am still the same person that I was when you loved me, but now that you do not, I am a different person in your eyes. You had the chance to get out of this relationship sixteen years ago when this came up at my mother's but you loved me and chose to stand by me. I am still Mike; I am still that person.'

The first judge to hear the case noted that it was 'curious'. That is something of an understatement. He found it extraordinary that the unusual physical characteristics were not discussed. Michael's case was that Ms J had known all along that he was a woman. The judge concluded that the sight of the birth certificate had such an effect on the wife that it was clear that she had not known the truth, but must have known that the husband was 'an inadequately or curiously formed male'. Ms J explained that she had never seen Michael fully naked, that he ensured she never saw him naked in the shower and that he exited from the shower backwards. An expert witness accepted that Ms J saw what she wanted to see and what she expected to see.

The defendant had sought to downplay the wrongfulness of his conduct:

> I took the [plaintiff] to [Lancashire] before we married and introduced her to my parents and sister. They said nothing to her about my operation. They asked me whether I had told the [plaintiff]; I said that I had not, but would tell her ... . We had sexual relations before our marriage. The question of my gender did not seem important to me and I never told her about it. I accept now that I should have done.

The defendant also referred to an incident when the couple had been to visit a sex shop in Soho where they had bought a 'penis extension'. The judge rejected this as evidence that the wife was aware of the husband's true sex. He accepted that she thought the aim was to add it to his existing false penis and it did not demonstrate that she understood the nature of his sex.

The law on determining a person's sex goes back to the case of *Corbett* v *Corbett* in 1970. There April Ashley had been born a man but had undergone gender reassignment surgery. She then managed to pursue a successful career as a glamour model. She married Mr Corbett. When he subsequently sought to have their marriage annulled on the basis that his wife was a man Mr Justice Ormerod had to determine how the law defines whether a person is a man or a woman. He decided that a person's sex is fixed at birth. In deciding a baby's sex, you consider their chromosomal, gonadal and genital features. If these all pointed to the baby being a male or female they could not change their sex by later having an operation. That case still represents the law although the Gender Recognition Act 2004 now allows a person to obtain a certificate which will confirm that they will now be recognised in their 'new sex' and therefore, in effect, change their sex in the eyes of the law.

By 19 August 1994 a decree nisi of annulment of the marriage of Michael and Ms J was granted. The ground of annulment was quite simple: the respective parties to the marriage were not male and female. The fact that the wife believed them to be so was irrelevant. English law was quite clear: marriage must be between a man and a woman. The primary issue was then whether the man could make ancillary claims against the plaintiff. She was wealthier than he was. The courts, of course, regularly make financial awards following a divorce, but the courts also have jurisdiction to do so when the marriage is annulled. In this case the court decided that, even though the marriage was void, it was still possible to make a financial order. The court rejected an argument that there was an absolute bar on him receiving an award due to the perjury he committed in order to get married. But nevertheless the court concluded that his behaviour towards the wife had been so bad that he should not receive any of her money. Crucial to that conclusion was the Court of Appeal's confirmation that the wife was unaware that her husband was a man. Lord Justice Thorpe stated:

66 *Many – and I am one of them – will find it quite astonishing that there was no single occasion in 17 years of life together when her eyes did not see, or her hands or her body feel, or her senses tell her that she was living with a man who had the genital formation of a woman, a man who did not simply have a small or deformed penis, but had no penis at all.* 99

In deciding that the husband had behaved so badly he should receive no money on the divorce Lord Justice Thorpe referred to the wife's statement. Ms J explained:

I am appalled by the deception which was perpetrated upon me. I cannot believe that the defendant was prepared to stand with me in church, before God, and make no disclosure when charged by the vicar to do so and to make vows to me and allow me to make vows to him. I would never contemplate entering into such a relationship willingly. I have been devastated by the disclosure of the

> defendant's true gender. ... On no account could I
> have contemplated placing myself in this position
> on 7 July 1977 and on no account would I have
> wished my parents to suffer the humiliation and
> distress which they would undoubtedly suffer by
> knowing that their daughter had entered into a cer-
> emony of marriage with a transsexual.

The dealings with the law for this couple did not end there. On 1 June 2005 Michael obtained a gender recognition certificate which acknowledged that he was, for the purposes of the law, now a man. At long last he had obtained legal recognition of the sex he always believed he was.

The couple again returned to the courts in 2006 with a dispute over the children. Michael did not want the children to be informed of the history of his sex and the cause of the marital breakdown. One issue which his application threw up was whether he was the father of the child. It was found he was not. In short, this was because he was not the biological father and he was not validly married to the mother at the time of the birth.

One of the many issues raised by this case is how to define what it is to be male and female. The biological difference between men and women is, in fact, far less than might be thought. In genetic terms scientists decoding the human genome have uncovered only seventy-eight genes that separate men from women. The total number of genes a person has is as yet unknown but it is thought to be between 25,000 and 30,000. The genetic differences are much less than had been assumed. Indeed the biological differences between men and women are not straightforward. This is especially so in the case of those with an inter-sex condition. These are people born with biological factors some of which are male and some of which are female. It has been estimated that up to 4 per cent of people are neither 100 per cent completely male or female. Indeed some people go so far as to suggest one can never draw a sharp line between male and female and it is better to regard there as being a scale of maleness and femaleness with people at different points along it.

To many people it is not the biological differences between men and women which are as significant, it is the behavioural ones. But as soon as that topic arises, it becomes easy to slip into stereotypes. When the BBC asked the general public for differences between men and women responses included the following:

~ Women know when all you want is a glass of wine, nodding sympathy and a good whinge. Men offer a solution.

~ Women know what to do when someone starts to cry. Men tend to shuffle out of the room mumbling something about doing the grouting.

~ Women pee together. Men do not acknowledge, let alone speak, to each other when peeing.

~ Men have no opinions about curtains.

These may reflect people's prejudices about men and women, rather than any actual differences. Certainly not all men are good grouters and not all women have excellent taste in curtains. O for the day when a person's gender will be as significant as their eye colour. But we are a long way from that idyll yet.

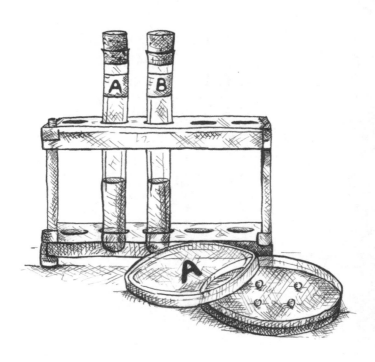

6

THE MIX-UP AT THE
IVF CLINIC

For those who have not experienced it, it is hard to imagine what it is like for a couple who are desperate to have a child and yet suffer infertility. Whereas in the past adoption may have offered the best hope for such couples, nowadays assisted reproductive services offer an alternative. For many couples, despite the use of assisted reproductive technology, no child is produced and the disappointment of the failed procedures, and their costs, adds to the pain of infertility. However, as this case shows, even when a pregnancy results, sometimes things can go horribly wrong.

Mr and Mrs A (as they were called in the court) were delighted when Mrs A became pregnant, following the use of assisted reproductive treatment at Leeds teaching hospital. No doubt, even more so, when it was discovered that she was carrying twins. However, when the babies were born it was clear something had gone wrong. They were of a different race to Mr and Mrs A, who were white. Dame Butler Sloss, the judge who later heard the case, explained:

"*After their birth it was noticed that the colour of the children's skin was different from that of Mr and Mrs A. Mr and Mrs A were obviously concerned and made inquiries. Subsequent DNA testing showed that whilst Mrs A is the biological mother, Mr A is not the biological father of the children. This was a great shock to them both, and I can only commend them for how they have responded.*"

The clinic had taken sperm from Mr A and eggs from Mrs A. The plan had been to use these to produce an embryo in the clinic and then to implant the embryo into Mrs A. Unfortunately, due to a mix-up the sperm of Mr B (a black man who was attending the clinic with his wife) was used to fertilise one of Mrs A's eggs. This was subsequently established by DNA tests. The case raised a host of possible legal issues. The one of most significance for the parties was who was the father of the twins. The case was clearly an emotional one. Mr and Mrs B were still childless at the time of the hearing.

There was no question about who was the mother: the mother is always the woman who gives birth to the child and in this case that was Mrs A. Under the law the woman who gives birth is the mother even if her eggs were not used to produce the embryo. But whether the legal father of the twins was Mr A or Mr B was a far from straightforward legal matter.

Mr A relied on a provision in the Human Fertilisation and Embryology Act which stated that a husband of a woman who became pregnant through assisted reproduction would be treated as the father, even though his sperm had not been used. That provision at first sight indicated that Mr A was the father. However, it only applies where the husband consents to the treatment that the wife received. Dame Butler Sloss concluded that Mr A had not consented to the treatment his wife had received. He did not consent to his wife being implanted with an embryo using Mr B's sperm.

That left Mr B. Mr B could be regarded as equivalent to a sperm donor. Normally sperm donors are not fathers of children, as long as they give their sperm to a licensed clinic and it is used in accordance with this consent. That is what the Act states. However, that provision did not apply in this case either because the sperm was not used in accordance with his consent. He only consented to it being used with his wife's egg.

Dame Butler Sloss concluded that none of the provisions in the Act provided for the scenario which had befallen this couple. She concluded that this meant that one went back to first principles. Namely that the man with the biological link with the child is the father. That meant that Mr B was the father of the twins.

So, the final conclusion of the case was that the twin's mother was Mrs A, but the father was Mr B. That was not the most convenient result, because it was agreed by all concerned that the children would live with Mr and Mrs A. But family law provides sufficient flexibility so that the correct result could be achieved. Mr and Mrs A could adopt the twins and that would mean they would become the parents of the children. Indeed this is what they did, although when making the adoption order the court required the couple to send Mr B twice-yearly reports on the children, including school reports, letters about their lives and photographs. In doing so, some acknowledgement was made of Mr B's links with the twins.

It is probably not surprising to learn that similar mix-ups have occurred in other countries. It is interesting that elsewhere the courts have reached the opposite result to that achieved in the English case. In one American case a white woman gave birth to a black child. She was ordered to hand the child over to the biological parents. That case was slightly different from the case involving Mr and Mrs A and Mr

B, because in the American case the woman giving birth had no genetic link at all to the child, while in our case the mother's eggs were used.

That throws open a wider issue. What makes someone a parent? Is it the genetic link between the parent and the child or is it the bond that forms between the mother and the child during pregnancy and birth? In a case such as the American one just mentioned, where one mother provided the egg and another one carried the child, the issue is thrown into sharp focus. Of course, the one answer that may be the most obvious is also the most controversial: to say the child has two mothers. That would be the mother whose egg was used and the mother who carried the child through pregnancy. However, so far English law and indeed most legal systems have stuck to nature's model: namely that a child can only have one mother and one father. If that is the approach to be adopted: is it genetics or nurture that matter for parentage? This is an issue about which people feel very strongly and whichever side a person takes they can find it difficult to understand the other side's point of view. (Just ask your friends how they would deal with a case of a woman accidentally being given another woman's egg.)

Mr and Mrs A's case led to a major review of the way licensed clinics handled sperm and eggs. Professor

Brian Toft produced a report on the mix-up in this case and he also considered three other 'adverse events' (i.e. mistakes) that had occurred at the same clinic. He found not a single cause of the problems but rather a combination of human error, poor management and inadequate systems. His report made more than one hundred recommendations for change. This included a requirement that:

> **Clinical and scientific inspectors check that clinics have procedures in place to double-check the identification of the individuals undergoing treatment, the sperm and eggs at the time of insemination and the embryos and the patient at the time of embryo transfer.**

Professor Toft found one cause of the problems to be inadequate funding of the Human Fertilisation and Embryology Authority which had meant it was not an effective regulator. Funding for the Authority had been the same in real terms in 2002 as it had been in 1990. This was even though the number of clinics that needed to be regulated had greatly increased. He recommended: double-checking of patient identifications at all stages of treatment; unannounced inspections of clinics; improved training for staff; and an alert system for untoward incidents. These proposals have been largely implemented. Nevertheless, between 2005 and March 2006, there were 140 incidents reported to the Authority, 91 of which were Grade A (the most serious). They included cases where embryos were lost after dishes were dropped or they were accidentally thrown away.

Six years after the case Mr and Mrs A spoke about it to the media, describing it as their 'nightmare'. They explained that the children were already asking questions about their skin colour. Most parents of children born using assisted reproduction do not tell their children about their origins. That will not be an option for this couple. Indeed they have been warned by psychologists that the circumstances of their birth could produce long-term psychological effects. The issues may be similar to the film *Toto le Hero*, where there was a fire in a maternity hospital and two mothers ran out with the wrong babies. As one boy grew up he was obsessed with the idea that he should have been raised by the other mother. Throughout his life he compared how the other boy had done in life and was convinced that but for the accidental swapping at birth his life would be so much happier.

Mrs A explained why the mix-up had affected her so much: 'The thought that I'd had children with a stranger felt like a violation in itself.' She also added, 'all we wanted was a family. Instead we were landed with a nightmare that will last for ever.' Mr A said he thought that many men in his position would have walked away but he did not consider that as an option.

Another sad recent case involving a mix-up in IVF treatment concerned a 13-year-old-boy who discovered the 'truth' about his parenthood after a six-year battle in the courts. He claimed that since the age of five he had doubted the man claiming to be his father was his biological father. Now his 'parents' had split up and he did not want to see the man. These doubts were correct in the sense that the child had been conceived at a licensed clinic using donated sperm from another man. It is interesting that the tabloids' response to this story was typified with the *Sun* headline, 'I always knew he wasn't my dad'. Yet in the terms of the law the man was the father and the sperm donor was not. So, in fact, the boy did know his dad, at least as the law defines a dad.

No legal proceedings were brought by Mr and Mrs A for damages. This is not surprising. The English courts have long taken the line that a child must be regarded as an unmitigated blessing. To award damages following a birth would send a negative message to the child that they were a burden to their parents. So only very rarely are the courts willing to accept that having a child is a loss which deserves compensation.

Finally, it should be noted that the cases discussed in this chapter have occurred in the context of assisted reproduction in clinics. There is quite an industry of 'do it yourself' assisted reproduction. At its crudest this happens with a friend being asked to provide sperm which is used in an attempt to make the woman pregnant, either via the traditional method or by the ubiquitous turkey baster. At one time *www.mannotincluded.com* offered fresh sperm for a price, although the website seems no longer to be operating. In the US there is a market in sperm with the cost depending on the intelligence, good looks and personality of the sperm donor. In the UK selling sperm is not allowed, although sperm donors to licensed clinics get a small sum for their expenses and troubles.

It is clear that questions over the definition of parenthood will continue to trouble the courts. With the announcement recently of the first pregnant man, family law is in for a tricky time ahead. This will not be the last case where the courts have had to struggle with the question: 'Who is my mum? Who is my dad?'

7

BEYOND THE CALL OF DUTY?

THERE ARE PLENTY OF BOOKS on 'how to be a best man' at a wedding. But you will face an uphill task finding a book on 'how to be an usher'. That is not surprising. It is not normally an onerous job. Beyond asking whether a guest is with the bride or the groom, and escorting the odd drunken uncle out of the reception, there is usually not much else to do.

Not so for the usher at Mr and Mrs T's wedding. Five years after the wedding the usher may have thought that his duties were long over. But his job was by no means finished. Mr and Mrs T contacted their usher with a most unusual request. They had been trying to conceive a child, without success. They sought infertility treatment, but again without success. So, they turned to a more traditional remedy. They asked the usher if he would have regular sex with the wife. A rented caravan was to be made available for use. Not perhaps the most romantic of venues, but no doubt it sufficed. The usher complied with the couple's request, indeed for some time, but to no avail. That was disappointing and, perhaps, surprising. The usher had four children already.

When the usher moved away from the town the couple resigned themselves to childlessness. But the urge to produce a child returned a few years later. By this time the couple, it seems, were getting desperate. The wife's biological clock was ticking away. The wife worked out that the weekend of 28 April–1 May 1993 would be a time when she would be particularly fertile. She decided to make it a blow out weekend. She had sex with her husband, the usher and three other friends all in the space of a few days.

This time it worked and the wife became pregnant. Of course, none of the men involved knew who was the father. Despite the statistical improbability, the husband was confident that he was the father. Indeed, that was the assumption on which the parents raised the child. It was not long, however, before rumours started to spread questioning the paternity of the child. The usher decided that he was the father. His fiancée became pregnant at about the same time as the wife. One might have thought that this would cause the usher to lose interest in Mrs T's child, but not so. The usher decided to broadcast the 'fact' that he was the father. He visited the mother and child on a few occasions and brought a teddy bear. He chose to publicise his paternity on his Citizen's Band radio. Not, you might think, a technique likely to reach a large number of people. More likely successes were his other methods. He paraded a placard beside a local taxi rank, where the husband worked. Later he stuffed letter boxes in the local villages with leaflets telling people he was the father. Not, one might have thought, the most likely way to persuade people of the truthfulness of what he had to say. Further, he asked the wife to marry him. She turned him down and the usher remained with his fiancée. Meanwhile, the husband was adamant that he was the father. He wanted to raise the child with his wife.

Predictably, perhaps, the issue reached the courts. The usher sought an order that DNA tests be performed so that his paternity could be proved. He then wanted to play a full role in raising the child. The mother and husband argued that tests should not be done. Under English law if biological tests have not been performed it is presumed that the husband is the father of any children born to his wife. Therefore, if tests were not performed in this case Mr T, the husband, would in law be the father of the child.

By the time the case came to court child T was aged seven. The central question was whether ordering the tests would be in the interest of the child's welfare. The arguments were straightforward. On the usher's behalf it was said that it was important for children to know their genetic origins. On the husband and wife's behalf it was said that if tests were done and it transpired that the husband was not the father then that would disrupt their family life. The father would feel uncomfortable about the child and the child might not regard the husband as his proper father. That would harm child T.

Mr Justice Bodey decided that the tests should be ordered. It was generally in a child's welfare to know the truth about his biological origins. In this case, given the rumours that had been spreading in the village, it would be inevitable that child T would find out about the doubts over his paternity. It was better that the truth were discovered now than wait until the child overheard rumours in the playground.

The judge accepted that the mother was emotionally clinging to the notion that the husband might be the father. Intellectually, however, he thought she knew it was better for child T to know the truth. Nor did the judge think this was a case where the husband and wife's relationship would be severely harmed by the discovery that the husband was not in fact the father of the child. The mother he described as a 'pragmatic, down to earth, sort of person'. A fair observation, one might think, given the facts of the case. Nor did he think that child T would feel any differently about Mr T if the truth were discovered. He quoted Lord Justice Ward's judgment in an earlier case who stated that if a child 'grows up knowing the truth, that will not undermine his attachment to his father figure, and he will cope with knowing that he has two fathers. Better that, than a time bomb ticking away.' The judge also noted that child T had a right to know who his father was under article 8 of the European Convention on Human Rights. All of these points indicated that a test should be done. The truth must come out. Although it has never been made public what the results of the DNA test were in this case.

The advent of DNA testing and the possibility of ascertaining 100 per cent truth about biological paternity has had an impact on the law of paternity. Previously, although blood tests could rule out a person as a possible father, they could never guarantee that a particular man was a father. Now proof is available. Indeed, ready access to paternity tests on the internet means that any questions over who a child's father is can be resolved discretely, and at relatively little cost.

Around thirty years ago a study was undertaken in Romford. Although it was not the primary aim of the study, it was discovered that 30 per cent of children living with a couple were not the biological offspring of the men they thought were their fathers. Such a study has not been replicated, largely due to the ethical difficulties such a study would raise. Many people believe that figure is higher than would be an average around the country. Maybe there is something special about Romford. Even if the figure is not representative of the nation as a whole, there can be little doubt that a significant number of children are raised in the false belief that a man is their father.

One of the more remarkable paternity dispute cases involved Boris Becker. It was said that mid-way through a Japanese meal he had sex with a Russian woman, Angela Ermakova, in a broom cupboard in the Nobu restaurant. There are two different versions of what happened in the cupboard. Angela is reported as saying:

> Boris pulled me into the broom cupboard. He became more and more passionate; to stop him when he was so excited was as impossible as stopping a high-speed train. I felt like Cinderella in a beautiful dream. Boris was like a radiant German knight.

Another version of events was that they only had oral sex. It was alleged that Angela Ermakova retained

Becker's sperm in her mouth and then used it to impregnate herself. That would be quite a feat. Did she not need to say goodbye?! Was she able to find equipment in the restaurant to get the sperm up towards the fallopian tube? Press reports quoted Dr Steve Brody who commented:

> It's possible for a woman to become pregnant with sperm inseminated into the vagina that's been ejaculated outside. ... When sperm is ejaculated it's a gel-like, viscous substance. Within five to 15 minutes it liquefies. This gel phase is probably a mechanism to protect the sperm cells in the initial phase of ejaculation. No one knows for sure why it comes out like this. It's only after it liquefies that it really becomes mobile.

Press reports suggested that Boris Becker only came to learn of Angela's pregnancy when she sent him a fax, stating: 'The project is quite advanced and is scheduled for launch at the end of next month. It would be really good to hear your comments and thoughts for possible participation. Perhaps you could call us.'

The Becker case shows that a man can become a father even without realising it! Indeed that case is one of several in which so-called 'sperm bandits' are claimed to have 'stolen' men's sperm to use to impregate themselves. Some have argued that in such cases it is not fair for the man to be burdened with the legal obligations of fatherhood. However, from the point of view of the child, he or she should not lose out on a right to have a father due to the unusual circumstances of conception.

The results of a DNA test can be traumatic. Where a woman has doubts whether or not her husband is the father, she should think carefully about whether tests are appropriate. One expert states:

> There is a genuine Pandora's Box in these sort of tests, that once you've opened the lid, you cannot close it again; once you know this, you cannot unknow it. You must ask yourself, 'if the result goes the way I'm not expecting, can I cope with that?' ... To be suddenly told – or to have a child told - that the person they thought was a parent isn't can have profound implications on their perception of who they are. And if people have an established family relationship, these tests can sever it for ever.

In England the former Home Secretary, David Blunkett, became involved in a bizarre paternity dispute. David Blunkett, who is blind, was said to have been having an affair with Kimberly Quinn while she was married to Stephen Quinn. By the time the case became public Mr Blunkett had ended his relationship with Kimberly Quinn, but he sought contact with her child William. Questions were also raised over her other son, Lorcan, who was a few months old. Mr Quinn was insistent that he was the father of the children. DNA tests were carried out and they demonstrated that Mr Blunkett was the father of William, but not Lorcan. The couple believed that the matter should be kept secret. 'It is deeply regrettable that Mr Blunkett breached our family's privacy causing further upset and press intrusion in our lives,' the husband stated. Of course, from Mr Blunkett's perspective it was not appropriate to refer to 'our family's privacy' because if Mr Blunkett was the child's father he was, in some sense, one of the family.

In the past, one suspects that in a case like this the truth would be swept under the carpet and the married couple would raise the child together as their own. But now that DNA tests can be so easily carried out, few will be able to resist discovering the truth. Especially when it is only a few swabs and a click on the internet away. Whether all this truth makes people any happier is, of course, a rather different matter.

8

THE MIRACLE BABY

" *This is a case about a young boy who is believed to be just one year old. I shall call him C. Although he was given a name in a religious ceremony, he does not have a true identity: that was stolen from him by a cruel deception perpetrated by adults who are involved in international child trafficking. Their motive is simple, one of the most base of human avarices: financial greed.* "

THAT WAS THE DRAMATIC OPENING of Judge Ryder's decision in relation to a most disturbing case. Mr and Mrs E were convinced that they were the parents of child C. Child C was described as robust, healthy and happy. Despite this there were two diametrically opposite applications before the court. An application was brought by the London Borough of Haringey for a care order. They wished to find alternative parents for child C. Mr and Mrs E were seeking a residence order because they wanted to raise the child as their own.

The central issue in the case was the circumstances of the child's 'birth'. Mrs E was aged thirty-eight and had lived in England for fifteen years. Mr E was aged forty-seven and had moved to England in 1996. Mrs E suffered from sickle cell anaemia which caused her pain and regular hospitalisation. The couple had not been able to have children of their own. They were charismatic Christians and joined a group called 'Gilbert Deya Ministries'. This group was a personal ministry started by a Mr Gilbert Juman Deya, who stated he was consecrated as an Archbishop in the United Evangelical Churches of America in 1992. The group's website contains a picture of Mr Deya meeting the Duke of Edinburgh and has this statement:

> We are the fastest growing Ministry in the UK and worldwide with a membership of over 34,000 in the UK alone. The vision originated from my home country, Kenya, in 1986. Our goal is to fulfill the commission of our Lord Jesus Christ by taking the Gospel into the outer most regions of the world. We believe in miracle signs and wonders, casting out devils, healing the sick and setting captives free in Jesus' name. We thank God for the visit of Her

Majesty Queen Elizabeth II and the support of His Royal Highness King Mswati III, former president of the Republic of Kenya Daniel T. Arap Moi, the viewers of our television programmes and the members of Gilbert Deya Ministries.

In the court Mr Deya described the group as an 'eclectic mix of traditional African custom and charismatic belief'. Of the many miraculous claims of the group the one that stood out for Mr and Mrs E was the power to facilitate 'miracle births'. These are said to arise without conception, the normal gestation period or even any scientific indications of pregnancy. Miraculous indeed. Mrs Deya, known as Mama Mary, counselled all couples seeking to have a miraculous baby.

The first day Mrs E attended the Gilbert Deya Ministries was a wonderful one for her. She believed that on that day she was cured of her sickle cell anaemia. She became convinced that through the Ministries God would grant her a miracle baby. She therefore arranged a meeting with Mrs Deya.

Mrs E gave birth to three 'miracle babies' between 4 September 2003 and 2 June 2004. The period of time may seem too short for three children, but remember that 'miracle babies' do not require the normal gestation period. Mr and Mrs E accepted that DNA tests on two of the children revealed that neither of them are genetically related to the children. Nor indeed are the children genetically related to each other. This they regarded as simply part of the miracle. Mrs E informed the court that at the date of the hearing she was 'pregnant' again, with another miracle baby.

The circumstances of the births appear to be as follows. Mrs E was prayed for in front of the whole congregation in 2002. It was prayed that this 'barren woman' receive 'the fruit of the womb'. Mrs E reported realising she was pregnant in January 2003. She experienced morning sickness, enlarged breasts and fetal movements. She went to see her GP, who referred her for blood tests and an ultrasound scan. These found no evidence at all of pregnancy. Indeed they indicated she was not pregnant. This did not convince Mrs E and she sought a second opinion. A consultant obstetrician and gynaecologist confirmed there was no evidence of pregnancy. She then sought the advice of Mrs Deya, who said it was normal for miracle babies not to be detected by western medicine. She advised Mrs E to go to Kenya to see a doctor there, who was more experienced in these cases. This Mrs E did. When she landed in Kenya she went straight to a medical clinic where she was given medication by a doctor.

Soon after taking the medication she 'gave birth' under the supervision of Dr Matano and a midwife called Esther. The facilities were primitive, with no running water and only a stretcher, no other equipment. Indeed the court heard that the clinic is not registered with the Kenyan authorities.

Mrs E gave birth to the three babies: A, C and G, at several clinics in Kenya, on different occasions. In each case she was suffering pain and taken to a clinic. Mrs Deya was present on the premises at all times. Mrs E was examined by a doctor who told her an injection was necessary. In the case of babies A and C after some 20 minutes she gave birth easily. She admitted that in none of the births could she see the moment of childbirth because of her position on the stretcher, but explained that in each case a child was held up for her to see and wrapped up and removed. Mrs Deya would then bring the child to her about half an hour later when Mrs E had recovered from the birth.

Sadly child A died shortly after birth, being very small and not breathing properly. Two days after that Mrs Deya suggested that Mrs E may still be pregnant and another baby may be inside. When they went to the clinic the doctor confirmed there was and shortly afterward baby C was born at a different clinic, some twenty-seven days after baby A had been born. C was born healthily and taken back to

England in October 2003. Mrs E registered baby C with a GP. There was no attempt to conceal baby C's existence. Indeed she was open about the 'birth'. The child was soon referred to the child protection team of the local authority. Meanwhile Mr and Mrs E were delighted and joyful at the gift of child C. There was clear evidence that they were good and loving carers of the child.

It was during the dedication service for C that Mrs E felt a kick in her abdomen and was convinced she was pregnant again. Her GP and hospital again informed her there was no evidence of pregnancy. Again she went to Kenya to 'give birth'. This time the birth took longer: five or six hours. The judge thought it significant that in the case of G's birth a Red Cross worker had been asked by Mr and Mrs E to provide independent evidence of the birth. After five hours the worker felt he could wait no longer. Shortly after his departure the birth took place. The judge described that as a 'coincidence that is too great to ignore'.

After G's birth the baby was left with Mr Deya, but soon removed by the Kenyan authorities. Mr and Mrs E, therefore, never got to spend time with baby G. As already mentioned, Mrs E at the time of the court hearing believed she was pregnant again. Needless to say her GP and hospital denied there was any sign of this.

In hearing the case the judge heard testimony from a colourful array of characters, giving evidence relating to the pregnancy. Of one the judge commented, 'Her evidence was a piece of theatre and wholly lacking in any credibility. [She] found what she wanted to find. She wanted and still wants to be in the limelight of attention but her evidence was no more than disjointed anecdotal supposition.'

Mrs E was adamant that the birth of baby C was a miracle. She stated that she knew of twenty-two miracle births that had occurred as a result of the Ministries. Eventually fifty families were to come forward asking to be tested to see if children found at the home of Mrs Deya were theirs.

One can understand the judge's difficulty at knowing how to deal with Mrs E's evidence. He concluded,

66 *I have regrettably also had to conclude that she is in part disingenuous, i.e. she knows or suspects that some of her account is not the truth, the whole truth and nothing but the truth, but she chooses to be silent about that. This is in distinction to Mr E who has an absolute, genuine and entire belief in his faith and accordingly has nothing to question. He of course has no independent knowledge with which to test his belief.* 99

Despite his unease about Mrs E's evidence, the judge faced a dilemma. On the one hand there was evidence that child C was being looked after by a devoted couple (Mr and Mrs E). Yet on the other there were strong suspicions that the child was not biologically theirs and had been handed over to them in unsatisfactory circumstances.

The child had been forcibly removed from Mr and Mrs E in November 2003. This, the judge thought, had been inappropriate. The hearing authorising the removal had taken place before a court without the parents being present. Such a procedure should only be used for emergencies and there was no sign this was such a case. The court was also concerned that the child's guardian, who represented the child's interests in the litigation, had not been able to assess the case independently because of her rejection of the parents' religious views. However bizarre a social worker might regard an individual's religious views that is not a reason for assuming that they will not make a good parent. The judge commented

66*It [the case] is not about a court's approval or disapproval of anyone's beliefs. It is not about the truth or otherwise of a particular religious belief. I do not presume to have that knowledge. Likewise, and despite some of the evidence that I have heard, this is not a case about the relative merits on the* *one hand of rational scientific theories of creation and life and on the other of charismatic belief, i.e. divinely inspired power and revealed truth.* "

The judge concluded his assessment of the facts in a brutally blunt way. No doubt he felt it was important that there be no doubts about what he believed:

" *I have come to the following conclusions on the evidence. Mrs E has never been pregnant. She did not give birth to A, C or G. In a cruel deception to further the financial ends of those involved Mrs E was deceived into thinking that she had given birth. She was seriously assaulted and a live child who had been born to another family was presented to her as her child. I cannot say where the child originated from. ... C's birth is not a miracle and he is not the child of Mr and Mrs E. On the balance of probabilities, the same must sadly be said of A and G.* "

The judge was equally blunt about Mr Deya's ministry. He accepted his powerful rhetoric, but also that Mr Deya taught that tithes should be paid to the church and that those who did not pay 'robbed God'. The judge thought the case was a sad example of the dangers of literal interpretation of religious texts in the hands of the corrupt.

None of this really helped the judge resolve the case. After all, as already mentioned, Mr and Mrs E were excellent carers. Even if the child was not truly theirs and they had been deceived (even if they had connived in the deception), that did not mean that it was not in the interests of the child's welfare to remain with the only adults the child had known as his parents. However, the judge thought that it was important that children understand where they come from and where 'in the context of life they belong'. If C was raised believing he was a miracle child and given a false view of his origins he would be harmed. He would discover the truth and this would cause his 'grief, loss and rejection'. This needed to be weighed against the benefit of the emotional warmth offered by the couple.

The judge wanted more efforts to be made to ascertain whether or not C's biological parents could be found in Kenya and in the meantime that he live in the care of the local authority, with foster parents. Subsequently, the attempts to discover the biological parents failed. Mr and Mrs E asked to be considered as full-time carers, although the local authority wished to give the child to a West Indian couple for adoption.

The case teaches many lessons. It demonstrates the desperation of those who suffer infertility and the great lengths to which they will go to find a child. It also shows how easy it is for hopes to become beliefs, and beliefs to become convictions. It seems Mr and Mrs E were desperate to believe miracle births had occurred, but it is hard to be persuaded that they really were convinced that the children were theirs. Yet the court's conclusion that the child should not be raised on the basis of this lie may be open to question. The vast majority of children born to couples who use donated sperm using IVF treatment are not told 'the truth'. Many children are raised by parents who tell them all kinds of lies about the world, their families, and their circumstances. These are not normally sufficient grounds to have a child removed. It may be that this case is not so much one about what is best for this child than an attempt by the court to deter child selling and to provide a strong disincentive to engage in it.

The characters in this case reappeared in the news later. In December 2006 Mr Gilbert Deya was arrested by the police. The Kenyan authorities had charged him with child trafficking. In November 2007 he was ordered to be extradited from the UK to Kenya. In November 2008 his final appeal to English courts failed. Bar an appeal to the European Court he will be required to return to Kenya to face charges of child trafficking.

Tragically the alternative care found for baby C by Haringey Social Services has been alleged to be lacking. There have been claims that six different sets of carers have been used. There have been claims that his adoptive parents were being investigated by a child abuse team after allegations that he was being beaten. The *Guardian* newspaper claimed there was a dossier on the abuse with a stream of concerns from anonymous phone calls. He was said to be screaming, unhappy, banging on walls and not eating. For this poor boy, despite the efforts of the courts and those involved, his earliest years have contained trauma and drama of a kind he could hardly comprehend.

9

DEVOTED FATHERS

THE MASKED MEN OF FATHERS4JUSTICE (F4J) have made quite a splash in the media. Their stunts have been eye-catching. They often involve campaigners dressing up as superhero figures. Batman and Robin scaled the Royal Courts of Justice in 2003; in the same year Spiderman scaled London Bridge; and in 2006 Father Christmas climbed on to the roof of a judge's house. In a major incident in 2004 purple flour bombs were thrown at the Prime Minister during Prime Minister's Questions at the House of Commons. This group and others have vociferously complained that the courts have failed to properly respect the rights of fathers following divorce. They claim that contact between fathers and children is not ordered often enough and that where it is ordered the courts are ineffective in enforcing their orders. Indeed the perception that the family courts are anti-fathers has become widespread.

But the issues surrounding contact between fathers and children are much more complicated than appear in the media. Let us start with the statistics on contact orders. In 2007 there were 73,267 applications for contact orders: 69,713 contact orders were made and 2,210 applications were withdrawn. In only 402 cases was the application refused. That is in fact a remarkably low number of refusals given the rates of child abuse and domestic violence. So, far from the perception that judges routinely refuse to make contact orders and deny fathers access to their children, in fact the courts are surprisingly willing to permit access. The real problems come in enforcing the orders.

The main focus of this chapter will be on a case where contact was granted by the Court of Appeal. This case highlights the difficulties a court can face. It involved a dispute between a mother and father over their child, R. The judge explained that the father was 'a 42-year-old fire officer' and the mother 'a 33-year-old Australian'. The implication of his comments was that the judge regarded being Australian as an occupation, which might, one supposes, take the idea of nationalism a tad far. Nevertheless, they had a boy, R, born in 1998. The father played an active role in raising the child until around May 2000 when the relationship between the parents began to deteriorate. Initially, after the separation R stayed four days and three nights each week with his father. However, disputes over contact arose and the matter was taken to court.

The dispute first appeared before His Honour Judge Lynch who clearly took a dim view of the father. He ruled that the father should have 'indirect contact'. This means that he could not actually meet the child, but he could send the child presents and cards. The father also applied for parental responsibility so that he would have a say in decisions about the child's upbringing, but this too was refused.

The reason the judge took a dim view of the father was this. It became clear during the hearing that the father had treated the mother with violence and was intimidating and harassing her. In fact the judge said he had engaged in 'deplorable conduct'. This was based on a number of incidents most of which occurred during times when the father was collecting or returning the child, having spent time with him. On one occasion it was found that the father threw a shoe that hit the mother. On another he forced his way into the house and ordered the mother to make him a cup of tea. He then pushed a hot tea bag into her face. On another occasion he hit her across the face and chipped her tooth, having seen her with another man. Yet another time he entered her house without permission, terrifying her. On another he filmed her at her workplace. The judge with some justification concluded: 'He has sought to use contact as a method of controlling her. If he carries on in this way he will break his link with his son.'

The mother reported feeling ambivalent towards contact. She recognised that child R should know both his parents but found the father to be 'intense, obsessive and demanding'. She claimed that the father sought to control her life. She was frightened of him. Even after the judge's hearing the father continued his campaign of harassment. He reported the mother to social services with complaints that the mother and her new partner were abusing child R. This, it was found, was malicious and based on unfounded allegations. The father appealed to the Court of Appeal, complaining that the judge had not properly dealt with his application.

The Court of Appeal confirmed that in deciding whether or not there should be contact the key issue was what was in the child's welfare. It was not a matter of which parent had behaved the best, or, even, who had behaved badly. All that mattered was deciding what was in the child's best interests. The Court felt that the judge had failed to bear in mind that the mother was ambivalent about contact and that both parents were seeking to work through difficulties. Terminating contact was seen as a 'Draconian' step.

The Court of Appeal were concerned that the judge had taken against the father and that the judge had viewed all evidence in this light. One example was that there was video of the father apparently saying goodbye to child R, giving a kiss and saying 'I love you very much and I am always here for you OK?' The judge said of this: 'It begs the question that as the child gets older the child is going to be wondering why it is the father is saying this. Why is it necessary for the father to keep saying this time and time again?' This seems a rather harsh view to take. The judge in the Court of Appeal commented:

> " *[The father's comment] seems to me to have been a most effective way of dealing with the situation and, given the intensity and passion of this father, a wholly proper and appropriate course of conduct. It is beyond criticism. Indeed, it is worthy of praise. The judge, however, is so adverse to the father and has formed such an unfavourable view of him that he does not give credit where credit is due. It is very difficult to see how else the father might have reacted. Had he handed over a screaming child to the lady who came to fetch him he would have been damned for failing to terminate that distress.* "

An important point in this case seems to be that R was relaxed and comfortable with both parents. He seemed attached to both his mother and father. The Court of Appeal decided that severance of the attachment with has father would be harmful for child R. The father was devoted to R and committed to him. The Court concluded that, with this in mind, contact between the father and son should take place.

The argument made by the Court, that the father may have behaved badly to the mother but was devoted to the child, is a controversial approach to take. It suggests that a father might show commitment and love to a child, while being abusive and threatening to the child's mother. Yet all the evidence we have indicates that domestic violence to a partner is harmful to a child. Indeed, harming a child's primary carer will harm the child. Being abusive to the mother, is also being abusive to the child.

The second issue before the Court was whether the father should have parental responsibility. This would give him legal authority to be involved in making decisions about R's upbringing. The original judge took this view:

"*As to the father's application for parental responsibility, I am satisfied that he would use it to help him interfere more in the mother's care of [R],*

which would only add to her stress and make it less
likely that she could properly care for [R]. I dis-
miss that application also. "

The Court of Appeal thought this improper. They
believed that the father should have parental responsibility given the degree of commitment the father
had shown to the child and the bond he had with the
child. Again critics of the Court of Appeal's decision
will claim that the father had demonstrated his will-
ingness to use his rights over the child to threaten
and abuse the mother. He should not therefore be
given greater opportunity to do so.

This case is by no means an easy one. From the
father's point of view we have a man who is committed to his child and of whom the child is very fond.
Although he had behaved badly in the past, this
should not mean the child is deprived of the benefits
of contact. From the mother's point of view the
father's violence and threats have shown a lack of
regard for her safety or the child's welfare. Any father
committed to the child's welfare would not behave in
the way he had towards the mother.

Yet for many fathers the separation from their
children is agonising. Bob Geldof has captured this
well in his description of what it is like for a father to
be separated from his children:

Everything can be tolerable until the children are taken from you. I cannot begin to describe the pain, the awful eviscerating pain of being handed a note, sanctioned by your (still) wife with whom you had made these little things, with whom you had been present at their birth and previously had felt grow and kick and tumble and turn and watched the scans and felt intense manly pride and profound love for before they were even born, had changed them, taught them to talk, read and add, wrestled and played with, walked them to school, picked them up, made tea with, bathed and dressed, put them to bed, cuddled and lay with in your arms and sang to sleep, felt them and smelt them around you at all times, alert even in sleep to the slightest shift in their breathing ... a note that will **ALLOW** you **ACCESS** to these things who are the best of you ...

In many cases it is not the making of contact orders which is the problem, it is their enforcement. Let us imagine the court has said that the father should see the child once a week, but when he turns up for the contact session the mother refuses to let him see the child. What can the court do? Well imprisonment is the normal punishment for breaching a court order, but that would harm the child and be likely to turn the child against the father for ever. Another option may be fining the mother, but that is likely to have the same effect. In 2006 the Adoption and Children Act was passed which enables the court to order the parties to meet to discuss the issue and resolve their differences. It is hard to imagine this approach working in most of these cases.

And even if the court were able to force mothers to hand their children over for a contact session it is likely to be a miserable arrangement for everyone. Contact between children and their non-resident parents works best when everyone involved works hard to make it a success. Then fathers can play a central role in a child's life, even if they live apart. Where there is irreparable damage to the parental relationship contact is often doomed to be a miserable few hours once a fortnight. The trouble is that the law cannot turn adults into angels. Judges hold no magic wands to make everyone perfect. They must deal with the messy humanity they have before them.

At the heart of this dilemma is research that suggests the reason why mothers refuse to allow contact after a court order is that they are fearful that the father will abuse them or the child. In these cases the judges must have concluded these fears are ill-founded. But the judges' conclusions will not change the mothers' minds, in which case they are unlikely to be amenable to threats. Even if they are, it is hard to believe in such a case that contact would be productive.

In a chilling survey by Women's Aid it was found that twenty-nine children were killed between 1994 and 2004 during contact sessions. Ten had been killed in the last two years, all of them by fathers. As this shows, the fears of violence the mothers have should not be too easily ignored. But this all makes the job of the judge so much harder. A father seeks contact, stating he loves his child. The mother opposes it, saying he is dangerous. If contact is ordered the judge may be putting a child in a dangerous position. If contact is not ordered a loving father may be denied contact with his child. What a terrible choice to have to make.

10

DIVORCING YOUR PARENTS

THE 1989 CHILDREN'S ACT ALLOWED children to bring cases to court in their own right. The tabloid press, predictably, got into a frenzy with cartoons suggesting that children would take their parents to court seeking orders that they did not have to eat broccoli. Or children introducing a stranger to their parents, with the words 'Mum, Dad, I would like you to meet my lawyer'; or indeed 'Mum, Dad, Meet my new parents'. It was a case of 'children's rights gone mad' claimed some. How long would we have to wait before we had the first case of a child wanting to divorce her parents?

In fact, few cases have come before the courts. Perhaps, despite the fears of journalists, children have more interesting things to do than go and see solicitors to discuss the problems they are having with their parents. Or maybe they just cannot be 'bovverred'.

One of the few cases where a child has gone to court involved a child, C, who was a few weeks shy of her fifteenth birthday. She had had a major falling out with her parents and went to court for permission to bring an application. She sought two particular orders. First, she wanted to go on holiday to Bulgaria with some friends, without her parents' permission. Second, she wanted an order authorising her to live apart from her parents. She managed to find a solicitor who was willing to act on her behalf. Her application was funded through legal aid. Legal aid would be available to any case involving a child, unless the child had significant sums of her own, or her application was devoid of any merit. Her parents appeared in court to oppose the application.

Judge Johnson, who first heard the case, opened his judgment by stating that it was a 'great pity' that the proceedings had come to court. He praised the lawyers in the case who had tried to encourage a reconciliation, rather than bring the matter to court. C was unhappy at home and had become good friends with a girl, A, who was also fifteen. A had invited C to join her family on a holiday. A lived with her fourteen-year-old-brother and father. They had all had a holiday together for two weeks and at the end of that C refused to return home. This led to C bringing the proceedings, hoping to have her current living arrangements formalised.

It was clear that one of the underlying issues in the case was the strong antagonism between C's father and A's father. Indeed, there had been a confrontation between the two men which had required the intervention of the police. It may even be that C was encouraged to bring the proceedings by A's father. He was clearly supportive of her doing so.

The judge noted that during the litigation the relationship between C and her parents had improved. There had been a disagreement over some personal belongings which C and her parents had negotiated satisfactorily. On one day C sat with her parents during lunch. That, the judge noted, was the first time that had happened for a long time.

The judge started his discussion of where C should live with some welcome realism. He noted that this was not a case where it was appropriate for force to be used to determine where the child should live. He accepted that in some cases that might be appropriate, but it was not here. C was fifteen and indeed it would be difficult to imagine how you could force a fifteen-year-old to live in a particular place, unless it was some form of detention facility. So in this case, C was living with A's family and they were happy for her to be there. There was not much C's family could do about it. *But* the judge did not think it appropriate to make an order confirming the current arrangement. Making an order would not give C any advantage. She could live with the family without an order. Indeed if an order was made and C changed her mind and decided to return to her family the matter would need to be brought back to court. In short, then, it was better not to make any order at all. The reality was that C would live where she chose and this was better left as a matter for the parties to discuss between themselves, than for the court to weigh in making orders. You might wonder whether the judge would have decided the same for a twelve-year-old or an eight-year-old? At what point does 'do what your parents tell you' cease to be an appropriate reply to a child who disagrees with his or her parents?

The issue over the holiday to Bulgaria was harder, the judge thought. Here, he could not take the route he had with residence and decline to make an order. C would need her passport to travel. The parents were currently refusing to hand it over.

The judge found that to properly resolve the issue on the holiday would require him to hear evidence from C and from her parents. The issue at the end of the day had to be determined based on the child's best interests. The judge noted that the issue had become one of overwhelming importance for C and her parents. He accepted the argument that allowing

C to go would move this issue to one side and might allow a long-term reconciliation. However, the judge concluded that the case should not proceed to a full hearing. Given the early stage of a rapprochement between C and her parents the judge did not want to jeopardise that by making a decision over the issue. The parties should continue to talk about it between themselves and find their own solution.

Judge Johnson did not think that going on holiday was the kind of issue Parliament intended children to be able to take legal proceedings about when enacting the Children Act 1989. He explained:

> *Parliament recognised the importance of children being heard in matters affecting their future. It does not seem to me that the jurisdiction is one that should be exercised to decide whether a child goes on a particular holiday or not. Indeed, for me to give leave in this particular case might, I think, be interpreted as an indication of the willingness of the court to entertain applications of children, even children of the age of C, on any matter in which they were in disagreement with their parents. In my view this jurisdiction is one which should be reserved for the resolution of matters of importance. This is not a matter that I regard as important.*

So C was not given permission to bring the application. If *where* a child goes on holiday is not thought sufficiently serious a matter for a child to bring to court, that is likely to be true of the many other kind of things a child might want to bring to the courts' attention: what food they have to eat; what they are allowed to wear; what time they must go to bed; whether they are to have a particular piercing.

A trickier case involved H who was also aged fifteen. His parents moved to France but he was not willing to move with them. He was very keen on dance and attended a dance academy in Bury St Edmunds run by Mr R. H wanted to live with Mr R while his family were abroad. Mr R was a married man with two children and three foster children. At first this arrangement seemed unproblematic. The social services were informed and had no concerns. But three months later events took a rather sinister turn. Mr R was arrested and charged with a serious sexual offence against a boy (not H). H stood by R, who denied the allegations. H did not want to leave Mr R and refused to live with his parents. His parents sought a court order to have him returned to them and an order that Mr R not contact H. Although the parents did manage to get H returned to them in France, he ran away and returned to England. At the time of the hearing he was living with a Mr and Mrs P but kept their location secret from his

parents. In August he took a large number of parac-
etamol tablets. Fortunately he was found before
serious harm was done. H had by then completely
rejected his parents. The parents became convinced
that H was under Mr R's influence. Their view was
supported by Dr Weir, a consultant psychiatrist. He
believed the relationship between H and R was detri-
mental to H. He wrote, 'I would say that R has
abused H's juvenile dependency over a period of
years in order to achieve a situation in which he is
largely in control of H's thoughts, feelings and
actions.' H disagreed with this assessment and
sought to be represented in the proceedings so that
he could make his own arguments.

The court acknowledged that there were concerns
about children being involved in litigation. If they
are allowed to be in court to make their own case then
they will hear parties give evidence, including their
parents. They will hear medical professionals and
other witnesses talk about them. This could be disturbing to the child. Also, the child might need to
comply with the requirements of confidentiality. So
if children were to be involved in court cases it is not
enough that they have sufficient understanding of
the issues; they need the emotional and moral maturity to be able to deal with the broader issues which
are likely to come up in the litigation.

In this case it was felt that H was a mature child and had the necessary understanding. He was regarded as already involved in the case. Even though the court was unlikely to agree with his arguments, it was right that he be allowed to put them to the court. Clearly what was influencing the court was that it was better for the court to engage directly with this particularly articulate and intelligent boy, and seek to persuade him that he was better off without Mr R. Not involving him in the proceedings was likely to alienate H and might therefore have been counterproductive. Even though he was permitted to act as a party to the proceedings the judge decided, not surprisingly, that H should not be permitted to live with Mr R.

One Canadian case comes closer to the kind of decision which people get worried about once children are allowed to bring cases to court. A twelve-year-old girl sued her father after he banned her from using the internet and stopped her going on a three-day school trip. These were punishments for going against his orders not to post photographs of herself on a dating website. She took the school trip matter to court and, indeed the case eventually reached the Quebec Superior Court. The Court held that the father had acted improperly. The girl had already been punished enough for posting the pictures.

There may well be more than meets the eye to this case. The girl's parents had separated and after the row with the father over the school trip the girl ran off to her mother. It was only then that her law suit was brought. The case might therefore really be a dispute between the parents with the child being used as a weapon in that dispute. It appears that both the mother and father needed to consent for the girl to be able to go on the trip and so the case may be regarded as much about resolving a disagreement between the parents, rather than a dispute between the girl and her father.

People's reaction to a case like this will vary. Some will see it as an example of state intervention gone mad. Are courts really an appropriate place for children to seek assistance whenever they disagree with their parents? If so we need to build many more courts! But it should not be forgotten that all kinds of petty and inappropriate disputes between adults reach the courts. If children are to be regarded as having the same legal rights as adults, should they not have the same access to the court system?

11

THINGS PARENTS DISAGREE ON

EVEN WHEN PARENTS ARE HAPPILY TOGETHER they frequently disagree on how best to raise their children. It is not surprising that when they separate the disagreements continue. However, rather than resolve them privately, some parents go to court to seek a ruling from a judge.

In 1996 a couple, who had been married for sixteen years, were divorcing. They had two children, a girl aged six and a boy aged nine. The mother went to live with a new partner, whom she intended to marry. The children lived with their father, although they saw their mother on a daily basis. Initially, this appeared to be a satisfactory way for the children to be cared for. However, an issue arose between the parents which came to disrupt the equilibrium.

The dispute centred on the mother's new partner. The father objected to two things in particular. First, the mother and her new partner had taken up naturism. They enjoyed living a nude lifestyle. Second, the mother and her partner partook in communal bathing with the children. Indeed there were allegations that the mother, partner and two children had all got into the bath together. One can only assume it was a very big bath.

As a result the father became unhappy with the children staying overnight with the mother and her new partner. In particular, he objected to the children being left alone with the mother's partner. He sought an order forbidding the naturist activities when the children were around. He also wanted the court to reduce the amount of time the children saw their mother.

At one point (presumably at the instigation of the father) the police and social services had become involved in the case. However, neither the child protection unit of the local authority nor the police were concerned with the situation. Still, the social workers advised to the mother and partner that, in light of the father's concerns, they should be careful and ought not bathe with the children.

The dispute over contact was brought to court and a court welfare officer was asked to prepare a report to assist the judge. Although there was evidence of the mother and her partner's nudity in front of the children and possibly communal bathing, this did not concern the court welfare officer. He recommended that the contact arrangements continued as before.

Judge O'Malley, who first heard the case, clearly thought the father was getting the issue out of proportion. He noted that there was no evidence that the new partner was a sex offender or posed a risk to the children. Indeed, he saw the father's application as an attempt to control how the mother was living her life in her home. He firmly rejected the proposal that if ever the mother had to go out and so the children were to be left alone with the mother's partner, they should be returned to the father. The children, the judge thought, would soon work out what was happening and it would send an entirely inappropriate message to the children about the mother's partner.

The issue still festered and the mother sought an order that the children's primary residence should be switched to her. The issue was heard by Judge Wigmore. He took a very different view to the nudity and communal bathing than Judge O'Malley. Indeed he thought it a major problem. He found that since the intervention of social services the mother and her partner had ceased their nudist and bathing activities. Nevertheless, the couple resented the restrictions on their lifestyle and did not believe they had behaved wrongly. Judge Wigmore stated:

“ *I must say I have found the attitude of [the mother] and [Mr E] somewhat startling, because it is my sad duty to deal with a number of public law cases where the local authorities are seeking care orders in respect of children and on not a few occasions we have children who are being taken into care for less than [the mother] and [Mr E] admit to having happened here.* "

When the Court of Appeal heard this case the President of the Family Division said of this comment: 'I have never come across such a case in my entire experience and I would be surprised if Judge Wigmore had himself.' That is the closest you will get to a senior judge telling off a junior judge. Surely the President was right. It would be hard to believe that nakedness or family bathing on their own would be enough to justify a care order.

Nevertheless, returning to Judge Wigmore's judgment, the President of the Family Division thought this was a grave matter and that social workers or psychiatrists would agree with him. He did not think the court welfare officer had taken the matter seriously enough. He realised that some people might think he was being a bit old-fashioned, but he felt that he was reflecting the view of experts. In the light of these concerns he did not think that the mother and her partner should have the children living with them, although the children should still see them regularly. He made it clear there must be no nudity or communal bathing.

The appeal against that order was heard by the Court of Appeal, and the President of the Family Division heard the case. She noted that in some senses moral attitudes in society have become more permissive than in the past, but in other ways less permissive. She gave the example, in relation to children, of an adult putting an arm around the shoulder of a distressed teenager. While in some circumstances that would be entirely appropriate, in others the adult will need to exercise caution in case the act is misunderstood. She noted the 'delicacy and sensitivity' that needed to be shown in relation to children. She also noted that families' different attitudes to a range of issues can be found. Showing a perhaps surprising knowledge of the nudist beaches of Britain, the President commented:

> "*Both on the beach and in the home some grown ups walk around nude – indeed you see it at one end of Budleigh Salterton Beach – and they bring up their children to do the same. Other parents pass on to their children a more inhibited approach to nudity. Communal family bathing is another example. This is often entirely innocent. In other families abuse may lie behind it.*"

She went on to explain that while some extolled the virtues of nudity, others were shocked by it. However, she added, 'In a happy, well-run family how the members behave in the privacy of the home is their business and no one else's.' It was this thought that dominated this case. The mother and partner should be left to live their private and family life as they wished.

The views of the President were more sophisticated than that, however. She noted that grown-ups who were less inhibited about nudity did run the danger of being misunderstood. It was especially important that new partners of parents should not raise the concerns of other family members. In this case the new partner had to realise that the children were not his and he should not behave in a way which was inconsistent with how the children had been raised. As she noticed 'children always talk'. She might have added, 'until they reach the teenage years', but she did not. At the same time, the President added that judges should be careful not to over-react to the less inhibited among us. It would be wrong to assume that those relaxed about clothing were sexual abusers.

In this case she thought it had been 'unwise' of the new partner to bathe with a boy aged nine who was not his child. The mother, she thought, would have been wiser not to suddenly change her attitude to nudity when her children had not been brought up to be accustomed to it. On the other hand, she thought the husband had over-reacted to what had happened. The President noted that the two junior judges in this case had remarkably different responses to the case, but 'judges are also human and they have their own feelings and indeed their own prejudices'. The Court of Appeal decided it was best if the issue over where the children should live be heard again by a new judge. The final result in the case was never made public.

One of the messages from this case is that judges are increasingly reluctant to set down what is or is not good parenting. In the past judges used to confidently declare what kind of parenting was good or bad for children. Nowadays the judiciary acknowledge there is a wide variety of styles of parenting. Certainly there comes a point when the standard of parenting is below what is acceptable, but for many day-to-day issues the courts just accept that there is no consensus on the best way to raise children.

That is true in relation to another issue which has troubled the courts on several occasions: circumcision. For many couples who have had a baby boy circumcision plays an important part of the child's welcome into the world. This is particularly so for Jewish and Muslim couples for whom the procedure has particular religious connotations. It marks the boy out as a Jew or Muslim. Occasionally the procedure is also arranged by those parents who believe it has medical benefits. However, many view the procedure as cruel and not within a parents' rights.

In one important case there was a dispute concerning a child J who was aged five. The father was from Turkey. Although he called himself Muslim, he admitted that he did not actively observe many of the tenets of his faith. The mother was English. Although she called herself Christian, she too admitted that she was not practising her faith. However, as often happens, religious differences that meant little to the parties during the marriage come to take on central importance when the couple separate.

The parents met while the mother was on vacation. It was a holiday romance. The mother returned to England a few months later and the couple were married in November 1992. They clearly cannot have known each other very well. Nevertheless they remained together until September 1996.

The father claimed that while she was pregnant the mother agreed that their son would be circumcised, but the procedure did not happen initially. The baby was raised in what the judge described as an 'essentially secular household'. Indeed the judge noticed that the father did not mix within Muslim circles or have any Muslim friends. Nor did the mother. After the separation the father sought an order requiring the son be circumcised. He explained that in his community seven was the normal age of circumcision for boys. That is why he had not had it performed earlier.

One argument raised by the father was J was a Muslim boy and should be circumcised as Muslim boys are. One expert explained why J should be regarded as Muslim:

> A Muslim woman may never validly marry a non-Muslim man. The law, however, allows a Muslim male to contract a marriage with a non-Muslim woman, provided she belongs to one of the revealed religions, i.e. Judaism or Christianity. Any child of such a marriage is a Muslim. It is a principle of Islamic law that the child of a Muslim father is always considered to be a Muslim.

The mother argued that J was Christian. The lawyer representing the child argued that the boy did not have a settled faith. Indeed he had been raised in a non-religious household. The Court of Appeal, when it heard the issue, rejected the argument that a new-born became a member of a particular religious group at birth. That may be how the parents saw it and how some faiths understood it; however, from the child's point of view the court stated, it was not until he became involved in religious activities and developed his own spirituality that he would be said to belong to a particular religious group. The fact that Muslim lawyers might regard the boy as a Muslim child was irrelevant to the secular courts.

A second issue which the court considered was whether there were non-religious reasons for performing the procedure. The judge accepted that there were particular medical conditions which made a circumcision advisable and child J was not suffering from any of these. The judge then referred to the opinion of a consultant doctor that the procedure is 'not pain free and there are potential risks both physical and psychological, which may be small but which are none the less definite'. More on the psychological harms later.

The judge noted that the parties, despite their non-observance of religion during the marriage, were both now raising religious issues. However, he found the mother's statement of her faith as 'pallid and unconvincing', while the father's was 'passionate'. The father said that he could not understand why the mother would object to circumcision. Circumcising child J would demonstrate and reinforce the son's relationship with the father. It would mean they would be 'the same'. If child J were not circumcised that would mean there would be a barrier between father and son. The judge accepted that child J's Muslim peers would be circumcised. An expert witness in the court explained how circumcision was an obligation for a Muslim father:

> ... an obligatory duty which should preferably be done at a tender age which helps the wound to heal quickly. It is a father's duty to carry it out as soon as possible. [If] he doesn't do it, while the child is still a minor, he would be failing in this duty.

It would be 'reassuring' for child J to know his contemporaries had been through what he had gone through. However, amongst his non-Muslim contemporaries, he would be in a minority. The father made what might be regarded as a strong point in that Christianity generally took no particular line on circumcision as a religious duty and certainly circumcising the boy would not be contrary to Christian teaching. However, not circumcising him would be contrary to Muslim teaching. On the other hand the court accepted that the mother would find it difficult to describe the circumcision in a positive light for child J. Rather than the circumcision being an event of celebration and fulfilment it would be a time of tension and stress.

The judge's conclusion was that the circumcision should not be performed. The boy was going to have an essentially secular upbringing and his contact with Muslims would be limited. In being circumcised he would not be in conformity with how his mother wished him to be raised or with the majority of his peers. So in no way would he be unusual or an outsider in not being circumcised. There were no medical benefits to child J and it would cause him pain and also carried a risk of physical and psychological harm. The operation would be stressful for the boy and it would exacerbate the difficulties between the parents. The barrister for the husband tried to argue that any emotional or psychological harm would be transient. In the father's words it was 'no big deal'. However, the Court of Appeal replied that, 'Fear, pain, despair or a sense of betrayal may all be transient in the temporal sense but still inflict emotional and psychological trauma that will burden a child for life.'

Some indication of the trauma that might arise is given by the mother who said

He [J] told me that his father talked to him about having his 'willy' cut and asked if he was still going to be able to go to the toilet. I had to explain to him that it would not stop him from weeing. This seemed to become more of an obsession to J as time went on and I could only presume that [the father] was constantly talking to him about this, which I did not think was very fair. It upset J ... J was very concerned at the effect of having the operation would have on him and I had to try to calm him down. To do so, I have obviously had to play down the effect of any operation upon him and I did not like not being able to be entirely honest with him.

In a rather different case Justice Barron made an interesting point. This case involved a father who was Hindu and a mother who was Muslim. The father was not very observant in his faith: he smoked; drank; ate beef; and had engaged in sexual relations before marriage. All of these were contrary to his religion's teaching. The mother was more observant in her religion. Again there was a dispute over circumcision of their son, with the mother for it and the father against it. Judge Baron pointed out:

66 *Circumcision once done cannot be undone. It may have an effect on K if he wishes to practice Jainism when he grows up. He has been ambivalent about his religion and is not old enough to decide or*

understand the long-term implications. It is not in his best interests to be circumcised at present. The Muslim religion, whilst favouring circumcision at 10 years and below, does permit of an upper age limit of puberty or later on conversion. By the date of puberty K would be [legally] competent and so he could make an informed decision. "

It was therefore concluded that it is best if the circumcision was not performed and that instead the boy could make the decision about it for himself when he was older.

There is still some debate over the benefits or otherwise of circumcision. At one extreme there are those who regard the circumcision of boys as a form of abuse. They argue that western society has decided that female genital mutilation (sometimes called female circumcision) is illegal. That is so even if the parents are acting for religious or cultural reasons. The dangers of the procedure and the impact it has on the woman's body and her ability to experience sexual pleasure is said to justify its illegality. Many feel the same about male circumcision. On the other hand there are those who claim that male circumcision has health benefits and that it is a widely practised procedure with important cultural and religious value.

The General Medical Council in its publication, *Guidance for doctors who are asked to circumcise male children*, summarises the debate about circumcision in these terms:

> Circumcision raises difficult questions about the rights and freedoms of individuals. Many people maintain that individuals have a right to practise their religion unhindered. Others feel that it is unequivocally wrong to undertake a surgical procedure, with its attendant risks, on an infant who is unable to consent. These are not solely medical matters and we do not think they can be resolved by the medical profession alone. They are matters for society as a whole to decide.

Time will tell whether society will continue to tolerate male circumcision or whether it will be decided that it is best for the issue to be left for the child to decide when he is old enough to do so. As it is irreversible, shouldn't it be for the boy to decide? It is his body after all.

12

A TRAGIC CONVICTION

WE GENERALLY ALLOW PARENTS to decide how to bring up their children. Indeed, when the government tries to tell parents what to feed children, what time they should go to bed, or how much television they should watch, the cries soon go up: we are entering a nanny state. But, it is generally agreed, there comes a point when the courts will overrule a parent's decision about a child.

There are few more tragic cases for a court than where there is a dispute over the medical treatment for a terminally ill child. In this case A was aged sixteen. The judge was required to give a judgment late on a Friday evening because the case was one of life and death and an immediate decision was needed.

Child A was the middle of three children. He was described by the court as having 'considerable athletic prowess' and being of 'average intelligence'. He appeared a normal, healthy child until, while on holiday, he started to feel stomach discomfort. Later these grew in intensity and one day, while watching his favourite football team, the pain became too much and he had to be taken to hospital. This, sadly, led to a diagnosis of leukaemia. The conventional treatment was to provide drugs which attack the leukaemia cells, but which also affect the blood generally and diminish the body's ability to produce more blood cells. This means that in addition to giving the drugs, blood transfusions are normally required. It was at this point the difficulties arose.

A and his family were devoted members of the religious group known as Jehovah's Witnesses. They believe that blood transfusions are forbidden by the Bible. Four verses are generally cited to support the prohibition:

~ **Genesis 9:4** – 'But flesh with the life thereof, which is the blood thereof, shall ye not eat.'

~ **Leviticus 17:12–14** – 'Any Israelite or any alien living among them who eats any blood – I will set my face against that person who eats blood and will cut him off from his people.'

~ **Acts 15:29** – 'You are to abstain from food sacrificed to idols, from blood, from the meat of strangled animals and from sexual immorality. You will do well to avoid these things.'

~ **Acts 21:25** – 'As for the gentiles who have become believers, we have sent a letter with our decision that they should keep away from food that has been sacrificed to idols, from blood, from anything strangled, and from sexual immorality.'

Although these refer to the eating of blood, the official line taken by the Jehovah's Witness faith is that the prohibitions include a blood transfusion. Other Christian groups do not interpret these verses in that way. Child A and his parents were devout members of the Jehovah's Witnesses and followed the official line. They were happy to agree to treatment for his condition. The one thing they would not consent to was a blood transfusion.

This led to an application to the court by the hospital. Mr Justice Ward was asked to authorise the treatment with blood products and with a blood transfusion, if necessary. The evidence before the court was that if blood transfusions were used the chance of success was 80 or even 90 per cent. In other words, it had a very good chance of success. However, if the blood transfusion was not used the chance of full recovery would be between 40 and 50 per cent. Without the blood transfusion it was more likely child A would die than that he would survive.

Jehovah's Witnesses are permitted to ask their surgeons to perform so-called 'bloodless surgery'. That is surgery which does not require blood transfusions. Although some surgeons are willing to do this, it is generally thought to carry far higher risks than surgery using conventional techniques with a blood transfusion. In this case the hospital did not think that bloodless treatment was a realistic alternative.

The official publication of the Jehovah's Witnesses, the *Watchtower*, suggests that if a Jehovah's Witness parent is asked 'Would you deliberately allow your child to die if blood would save it?', they should answer 'I would demand that medical science do everything possible to save my child's life short of giving it blood'. It is not known how many Jehovah's Witness children have died as a result of this teaching. Undoubtedly some have and the Jehovah's Witness publication *Awake* in 1994 displayed the photographs of twenty-six children with the caption 'Youths Who Put God First'. It proudly declared: 'In former times thousands of youths died for putting God first. They are still doing it, only today the drama is played out in hospitals and courtrooms, with blood transfusions the issue!'

Although this is the official doctrine of the group, it is not clear how many Jehovah's Witnesses do adhere to it. One study in 1982 found 12 per cent of them said they would not follow the official doctrine if it would lead to death. The doctrine has caused a particular problem for haemophiliacs, whose treatment requires the use of blood products. In 1975, with haemophiliacs in mind, the doctrine was officially changed to allow them to use clotting factors derived from blood. The explanation that was offered was that because an extract from blood, rather than the whole blood, was used, it fell outside the general prohibition.

There is a group known as the Associated Jehovah's Witnesses on Reform of Blood, which campaigns to change the attitude of the group towards the use of blood transfusions. They argue that the doctrine is not supported by a large number of Jehovah's Witnesses. Further it leads to needless death of the group's members.

Mr Justice Ward acknowledged that this was an 'excruciatingly difficult case'. The boy and his parents fervently believed that the use of blood products was sinful and this could affect his eternal salvation. The doctors believed use of these blood products was essential to save his life.

The court's analysis started with the 'fundamental principal' that an adult with mental capacity has the absolute right to refuse treatment. This is so even if, without the treatment, they will die. The same principle does not, however, apply to children. There the law is a bit more complex.

In one important case (the 'Gillick' ruling) the House of Lords held that a child under sixteen could consent to medical advice or treatment if he or she was sufficiently mature to understand the relevant issues. That case concerned providing contraceptive advice and treatment. Their lordships held that a mature child could consent and indeed her parents did not have to be told about the treatment.

The case of child A was, however, rather different from the Gillick case, because it involved a situation where the child was objecting to treatment, rather than wanting to consent to it. But you might think that should make no difference. If a child is regarded as sufficiently mature to make the decision, as mature as an adult might be, we should give them the same right an adult has. That includes not only the right to give effective consent to treatment, but also to refuse to consent. But in law these are regarded as different cases. The law wants to ensure that a child receives the treatment he or she needs. By allowing children to consent to treatment doctors can provide treatment which a parent would object to. But where children are refusing to consent, respecting their views would mean they are not getting treatment they need. So there their refusal can easily be overturned to ensure they get the treatment which will benefit them.

So one key question in this case was whether or not A was sufficiently mature to be able to make the decision to refuse treatment. Justice Ward thought not. He provided four reasons.

First, child A did not understand 'the whole implication of what the refusal' of the treatment involved. The judge accepted that child A was of 'obvious intelligence' and was able to have a 'calm discussion' of the implications of his refusal. Further he was aware he would die. However, child A did not comprehend the pain he would suffer without the treatment. In particular the increasing breathlessness he was likely to suffer and the fear that that would generate.

Second, the judge found that A did not appreciate the distress he would suffer 'as he, a loving son, helplessly watches his parents' and his family's distress'. Third, the judge though child A would not appreciate the extent of his family's suffering as they watched him die. Fourth, the judge said this:

> " [H]is volition has been conditioned by the very powerful expressions of faith to which all members of the creed adhere. When making this decision, which is a decision of life or death, I have to take account of the fact that teenagers often express views with vehemence and conviction – all the vehemence and conviction of youth. Those of us who have passed

beyond callow youth can all remember the convictions we have loudly proclaimed which now we find somewhat embarrassing. I respect this boy's profession of faith, but I cannot discount at least the possibility that he may in later years suffer some diminution in his convictions. There is no settled certainty about matters of this kind. "

This final reason is controversial. A had been strongly influenced in his religious beliefs by his parents and the court could not be certain that they were his own. Inevitably a child will be influenced by their upbringing and the views of their parents. This is true of most adults. If a child is to be found to lack capacity to make a decision because he or she is still influenced by her parents then that would mean nearly all children would automatically be found to lack capacity. It may be argued that religious beliefs is an area where children are particularly sensitive to being 'brain washed' by their parents. That is a controversial suggestion and may be true just as much if the parents are atheist as if they are religious.

Having decided that A lacked the capacity to make the decision the court was required to make the decision about what treatment he should receive. This was to be determined based on an assessment of his best interests. That may sound like a straightforward test and you might think that it is obvious that it is in his best interest to live, but the issue is complex.

As Justice Ward noted, in deciding what is in a person's best interests their own views must be taken into account. In this case that involved bearing in mind that A would be forced to have blood transfusions against his wishes. Indeed he would be forced to endure something he regarded as sinful. The judge was referred to a Canadian case where it was found that the child so opposed the treatment that she would 'fight that transfusion with all the strength she could muster. She would scream and struggle, pull the injecting device out of her arm and attempt to destroy the blood in the bag over her head'. Justice Ward did not think that would happen in this case. Child A, he thought, would protest, but not to that extent. In the end he concluded that the emotional trauma of being forced to have the treatment would be outweighed by the benefits of staying alive.

It is necessary when thinking about best interests to consider what is in the best interests of a particular individual. So, the judge said the question was what is best for A, 'given his own position as a boy of growing maturity living in the religious society that he does'. This meant it had to be borne in mind that the religious community he lived in would regard the blood transfusions as sinful.

It is also necessary to give due weight to the views of parents. Normally in our society we allow parents to raise children in whatever way they wish. We do not overrule parents' views on the basis that they are a minority belief. Indeed, unless the parent is causing the child significant harm the state will not intervene in the way parents raise a child. In relation to that Justice Ward referred to a statement by his American counterpart Justice Holmes who stated

> *Parents may be free to become martyrs themselves, but it does not follow that they are free in identical circumstances to make martyrs of their children before they have reached the age of full and legal discretion when they can make choices for themselves.*

Justice Ward, in concluding his analysis, said, 'One has to admire – indeed one is almost baffled by – the courage of the conviction that he expresses. He is, he says, prepared to die for his faith.' Nevertheless, 'the welfare of A, when viewed objectively, compels me to only one conclusion, and that is that the hospital should be at liberty to treat him with the administration of those further drugs and consequently with the administration of blood and blood products.'

These cases are made all the more difficult due to the belief among some Jehovah's Witnesses that if the blood transfusion is compelled by the court it is no longer sinful. It may be that parents in many cases feel compelled by their faith to object vehemently to the treatment, while secretly hoping the court will override their objections. That ambiguity makes the decision for judges in these cases even harder.

The story did not finish there. Child A was given the blood transfusions against his will for the next couple of years. Once he reached the age of eighteen he had the right to refuse the transfusions. This he did and soon afterwards he died. One is left with the concern that in retrospect all the court had done was force treatment upon this devout young man, postponing, but not avoiding his death. The difficulty in cases of this kind is that you never know whether by the time the child has reached the age of eighteen he or she will say 'Thank goodness you did not listen to me when I was younger; I now realise how foolish I was to refuse the blood transfusion'; or, 'You have abused me for long enough, now I am an adult and have the right to refuse treatment. You must let me die.'

13

WHAT'S IN A NAME?

IT IS QUITE EXTRAORDINARY how many cases have come before the courts involving disputes over the name of a child. It may be thought that the child's name is of little importance for the child in the grand scheme of things. Whether the child has the name of Sarah Smith or Jane Jones doesn't really matter does it? However, it is clearly an issue about which parents feel strongly. Men especially seem to feel that if the child does not have their surname then the child is not really their's. Women, generally, have less attachment to surnames. This may be because women in the UK commonly lose their surnames on marriage and adopt their husband's.

English law on surnames is astonishingly informal. A person's surname in law is simply that by which she or he is customarily known. This does not have to be the name on their birth certificate. I could be Jonathan Smith one year and Jonathan The Man, next year. A person can sign a deed poll to provide formal evidence of a change from the registered surname, although they don't need to. There is no need to notify any formal state authority before one starts living under a new name. However, that may change if identity (ID) cards are introduced.

Of course parents traditionally take a long time deciding what name to use for their child. When Jordan and Peter Andre announced the name of their daughter, Princess Tiáamii, they felt it necessary to justify their decision. The name Princess was said to convey the meaning that the child was 'their princess' and the name 'Tiáamii' was a combination of the names of their mothers: Amy and Thea. Although Jordan explained, 'We've put an accent over the first A to make it more exotic and two Is at the end just to make it look a bit different'. The couple explained that they had considered using the name Tinkerbell, but decided not to use it because too many celebrities used that name for their dogs.

Until fairly recently in historical terms surnames were unknown, although names of some kind seem to have been used from earliest times. Until the mid-part of the middle ages people generally only had given names. Surnames appear to have grown from the difficulty of there being too many people with the same given name and performed the role of distinguishing between them. In the earliest times the surname was bestowed by the community. It might refer to some characteristic of the person or the place where they lived. Hence, 'Hill' and 'Short' are some of the earliest names. The person's job or personality was another popular inspiration. Hence names such as 'Carpenter' or 'Hardy' were developed. So, in their origins surnames were personal descriptions, rather than a reference to a family tie. It appears to have been the Normans who first introduced the custom of naming sons after fathers. But that did not become a universal practice until much later.

Nowadays, there is no restriction on what names parents can select. The child's surname does not need to be one of their own. Parents' imaginations can run riot. I am reliably informed that Bud Weiser, Iona Frisbee, Lou Zar, Shanda Lear, Richard Head and Abbie Birthday all exist and have their parents to thank for their names. In one case in New Zealand the public authorities took a case to court after the parents called their child 'Talula Does The Hula From Hawaii'. The judge decided that the name was a form of abuse and the girl was placed under the guardianship of the court. The judge noted the choice of such a name was part of a wider phenomenon. He referred to other cases in New Zealand where a child had been called 'Number 16 Bus Shelter' and twins had been given the names, 'Benson' and 'Hedges', and 'Fish' and 'Chips'. Some celebrities' children rebel: Zowie Bowie has said he wishes to be known as Duncan.

Judges in the family courts in the UK tend to take a strong line against hearing disputes on irrelevant issues. It is, for example, almost unknown for courts to hear disputes over pets. However, the judiciary clearly think names are important. Lord Jauncey elaborated on what he regarded as the significance of a surname:

> "*A surname which is given to a child at birth is not simply a name plucked out of the air. Where the parents are married the child will normally be given the surname or patronymic of the father thereby demonstrating its relationship to him. The surname is thus a biological label which tells the world at large that the blood of the name flows in its veins. To suggest that a surname is unimportant because it may be changed at any time by deed poll when the child has attained more mature years ignores the importance of initially applying an appropriate label to that child.*"

This quotation is interesting for several reasons. It is notable that the child is referred to as 'it', reflecting an ownership view over a child. The blood in the child's body is described as 'the blood of the [father's] name'; rather than being simply the child's blood. Or even (if one wanted to see the issue in the judge's terms) the blood of *both* parents.

Of course the name is really of symbolic significance. What is being fought over is in itself rather minor, but the issue it reflects may be important. The fight over a name is often the tip of an iceberg. Typical of the kind of cases heard by the courts is one involving a child called Gemma. At the date of the hearing she was five. Her parents sadly separated just before her second birthday in acrimonious circumstances. Although when she was born the girl was called Gemma C (the father's surname) shortly after the separation the name was changed to Gemma H (the mother's surname). The father objected to this vociferously and strongly, although he had not found out what had happened until several years later. The father was seeing Gemma regularly, but he clearly regarded the change in name as an attempt to undermine his position as a father.

The judge who first heard the case focused on four factors. First, that for the past two years the girl had been known as Gemma H and if that were to change it would be disruptive. Second, that 'eyebrows would be raised' if Gemma were to attend school with a different name from that which her mother had. Third, the father had chosen not to marry the mother and had he done so his case would have more merit. Fourth, although requiring a child to have a father's surname could reinforce the link between the child and father, that was not needed here as the child was seeing the father regularly.

The Court of Appeal were not convinced by the strength of these arguments. They noted that 'The breakdown in relationships is now of such magnitude that there is nothing at all unusual in children having names different from their mother.' So the eyebrow raising argument was not a persuasive one. They also thought that the refusal of the father to marry the mother was an irrelevant factor. The argument that the link with the father did not need to be reinforced by the surname was also rejected. The surname could help reinforce the paternal link whether or not there was contact.

The Court of Appeal stated that changing the name of a child was a major step. The name represented a link with the father and if the child ceased to bear the father's name that would understandably harm the child. Having the father's name will not be harmful and will 'advance her knowledge in knowing who she is'.

The Court of Appeal went back to the basic principle that the court needed to determine what was in the best interests of the child. Gemma herself was too young to have views that could be taken into account, but she had learned to write her name (as Gemma H) and she had written that in all her books. Even though the court decided that the mother had behaved badly in changing the name, the court felt it had to take the situation as it found it. The child was being raised by a mother who was strongly of the view that H was the correct surname and forcing the mother to use C could be unenforceable or poison the relationship between the child and father. The 'unhappy conclusion' the court reached was that Gemma should continue to be known by the surname H.

As the courts in Gemma's case demonstrate there is a limit to what the courts can do in regards to names. The court might order that a child be known by a particular name, but they cannot control how the child is known day to day. This is especially true with an older child who has strong views on what they want to be called.

Not all judges have been as sympathetic as the Court of Appeal was in this case to fathers who want their children to retain their surnames. Baroness Hale has written:

"I return to the issue of names. It is also a matter of great sadness to me that it is so often assumed, and

*even sometimes argued, that fathers need that out-
ward and visible link in order to retain their
relationship with, and commitment to, their child.
That should not be the case. It is a poor sort of
parent whose interest in and commitment to his
child depends upon that child bearing his name.
After all, that is a privilege which is not enjoyed by
many mothers, even if they are not living with the
child. They have to depend upon other more substantial things.* "

Bob Geldof has responded to these comments with
characteristic vigour. He noted the:

> judicial disapproval for a man who objected to a
> woman who wished to change the child's surname.
> 'A poor sort of parent' is what this unfortunate was
> called, whose child would at least know who she
> and her father were before the past and her identity
> were stripped, like a Stalinist photograph out of
> her family's history. He was not allowed even to
> give her his name. Her family name. So a man is to
> be stripped of even that. He is to be utterly
> expunged from the past.

Some commentators have seen this whole issue as
male obsession with names. They say that men

expect their wives to take on their surnames on marriage and then their children to have their surnames too. This is therefore a thinly disguised claim to ownership of his 'tribe'. It is unlikely that many men explicitly think of surnames in this proprietorial way, but they may do so subconsciously.

There is hope. In one recent case the court produced a solution which may provide the way ahead for disputes of this kind. That is that the child have a double barrelled surname, with one surname being the choice of the mother and one the choice of the father. This seems a ready solution and if adopted as a general norm it might reduce litigation over many of these cases. Or maybe not. Perhaps there would still be arguments over which name would go first. After all, some parents will pick on anything to make an argument.

14

WHICH OF THEM DID IT?

PROFESSIONALS WORKING IN THE AREA of child protection must feel they cannot win. The blood of tabloid writers boils when they discover that children are being taken away from parents for inadequate reasons and social workers are blamed for prying into other people's lives. Yet if they don't intervene social workers are castigated for leaving a child in an abusive situation. After the event it can be all too easy to see whether social workers were over- or under-reacting. But at the time it can be impossible to tell. I wonder sometimes how social workers are able to sleep at night. There certainly needs to be far greater recognition of the importance of the work they do and the genuinely difficult decisions they have to make. The case which is the focus of this chapter is an example of the problematic cases which courts and social workers have to deal with.

The House of Lords in this case had to deal with a serious and difficult issue, that of child abuse. The basic facts are all too common. A local authority seeks to remove a child on the basis of suspicions that the child is being abused. The parents vehemently deny allegations of abuse. Take the decision that the child should be left with the parents and the judge may be leaving a child to suffer years of abuse or neglect. Take the decision to place the child into care and, if the judge has got it wrong, he or she is depriving the child of the right to be raised by her parents and has branded the parents as abusers. In many ways the stakes in these cases could hardly be higher.

The Children Act 1989 allows children to be removed from their parents under a care order only if the so-called 'threshold criteria' are met. These require, first of all, that the child be suffering or is likely to suffer significant harm. Second, that the harm is attributable to 'the care given to the child … not being what it would be reasonable to expect a parent to give'. These conditions mean that even though a local authority may be persuaded that a child is suffering some harm, if it is not significant then the child may not be removed. So a child may be being fed an unhealthy diet, but unless this is causing serious health problems the child should be left with the parents. It is also notable that the child can only be removed if the significant harm is related to the care the child is receiving. This is important, because a child may be suffering significant harm due to, say, a disability or bullying at school, but that does not necessarily justify the intervention of the law.

The application of these principles in one case reached the House of Lords. The case involved child A who was just under one year old when she was taken into care. Her parents lived together. The father was in full-time employment and her mother, as is so common these days, was keen to return to work soon after the baby was born. Indeed the mother did so when the child was but three months old. While she was at work a child minder took over the care of the child. All seemed well and this modern arrangement appeared to be working. But after two months with the child minder it was found that A had suffered a serious head injury. The experts found this to be non-accidental, meaning that it was done deliberately, probably through violent shaking. The local authority were informed and immediately applied for a care order in respect of A and the child minder's own daughter (B). When A left hospital she was placed with foster parents.

When the case came to court the judge faced a dilemma. It was beyond doubt that someone had seriously harmed baby A. What was unclear was who had done it. The judge concluded that there were three suspects: A's mother; A's father or the child minder

(B's mother). All of them denied harming the child. His Honour Judge Gee described the dilemma:

> "If the criteria are met and orders are made I am exposing one child to the possibility of removal from parents who are no risk and have done no wrong ... If the applications are dismissed then I will undoubtedly be causing one child to be returned to a parent or parents, one or both of whom are an obvious and serious unassessed risk."

His point was that if Mr and Mrs A had caused the harm to baby A, then a care order in respect of child B could not be justified. But if the child minder had harmed the child he thought a care order in respect of A could not be justified as her parents would not be responsible for the injuries. This led him to conclude that the care orders should not be made. He could not conclude that A's parents had caused her injuries and he could not conclude that B was at risk of suffering significant harm. It was best, therefore, not to make an order.

The Court of Appeal saw the case rather differently. Their emphasis was on the dangers of children being left in a harmful situation:

❝ *With the rise in broken marriages and unmarried relationships, and the economic pressure on mothers to remain in employment even while their children are young, the task of caring for children is often shared between parents who are living apart, grandparents and other relatives, and official and unofficial child minders. Where the task is shared in that way and a child suffers serious harm through lack of proper care, that child must not be left at risk simply because it is not possible for the court to be sure which part of the care network has failed.* ❞

The issue went on to the House of Lords.

Lord Nicholls who heard the appeal said that there would be some cases where there would be no difficulty in applying the law. First, where it was clear either the mother or father had harmed the child, but it was not clear which had. In such a case he thought the threshold criteria were met and the child could be taken into care. Second, where either the parents or the child minder had harmed the child, but that if it was the child minder, the parents could be said to be at fault for not supervising or selecting the child minder. In such a case the parents were at fault either because they harmed the child themselves, or because they had failed to protect the child from the child minder. But it was a third kind of case their lordships were dealing with: the harm had been caused by the child minder or the parents, but there was no evidence that the parents had been at fault in their selection or supervision of the child minder. This meant that if it had been the child minder who had caused the harm, the parent might not be to blame. Could it be appropriate to remove a child from parents who may therefore be blameless?

'Yes' was the answer from the House of Lords. The approach taken by His Honour Judge Gee (the first judge) would leave a child who had received repeated non-accidental injuries without protection, simply because it was not possible to determine who had caused the injury. Lord Nicholls thought it could not be right that 'the child's future health, or even her life, would have to be hazarded on the chance that, after all, the non-parental carer rather than one of the parents inflicted the injuries'. As he noted it is increasingly common for children's care to be shared between parents, relatives and others employed to care for a child. If a child was injured and all those involved just kept mum, Judge Gee's approach would mean a child could not be protected. But their lordships concluded that it would be too dangerous for a child to be left in a situation where someone involved in caring for the child had harmed her. In this case, therefore, the Court were entitled to make an order removing the children.

In short, the decision means that even a blameless parent can have his or her child taken into care. The choice, as their lordships saw it, was between accepting the unfairness to such a parent against the danger for a child left in a dangerous situation. Between these two it was better to protect the child than the parent.

A rather different issue arose in another case where the local authority were concerned about parents with learning difficulties who were raising a girl aged ten and a boy aged seven. The mother had several disabilities. After testing her a psychologist concluded: 'On all these scales [the mother] was at or below the first percentile. She requires assistance to perform all her household or nurturing tasks. She is dependent on support from her husband and three different care workers who assist her during the week. Her greatest skills are practical and her weakest verbal.' Further, there were concerns that in the past the father had allowed a paedophile to visit the home, where he had abused the girl. There were also unproven allegations that the father had whipped the children with belts and proven allegations of domestic violence. The children were taken into foster care, but stated they wished to be with their parents. The judge found that the threshold criteria had been met.

The most interesting part of the Court of Appeal's judgment, which ordered that the case be reheard, were the comments that:

> *family courts do not remove children from their parents into care because the parents in question are not intelligent enough to care for them or have low intelligence quotas. Children are only removed into care (1) if they are suffering or likely to suffer significant harm in the care of their parents; and (2) if it is in their interests that a care order is made. Anything else is social engineering and wholly impermissible.*

The case was indeed reheard where some similar sentiments were issued by Judge Hedley who held:

> *society must be willing to tolerate very diverse standards of parenting, including the eccentric, the barely adequate and the inconsistent. It follows too that children will inevitably have both very different experiences of parenting and very unequal consequences flowing from it. It means that some children will experience disadvantage and harm, while others flourish in atmospheres of loving security and emotional stability. These are the*

consequences of our fallible humanity and it is not the provenance of the state to spare children all the consequences of defective parenting. In any event, it simply could not be done. "

He went on to make it clear that 'at least something more than the commonplace human failure or inadequacy' was required. In this case 'certainly they have suffered harm; certainly it is likely they will do so in the future and certainly that has been and will be attributable to the parenting they receive'. Nevertheless, there had been insufficient evidence to justify taking the children into care.

The case raises some difficult and interesting issues. Should we accept that treatment of a child of parents with learning difficulties will not meet the threshold criteria, while the same treatment of a child by parents without learning difficulties will? Should there be minimum standards of parenting which children are entitled to expect regardless of the personal characteristics of their parents? Or is the lesson really to be learned from cases such as these that parents with difficulties need special support and help from society, so that they can become adequate as parents?

The issue might be broadened out. There are certain categories of parents where there is a high likelihood that their children will suffer significant harm: parents who are drug users or alcoholics; parents who have committed serious crimes; parents who have severe intellectual impairment. With such parents would it not be better to remove their children at birth and have them adopted, rather than wait for the child to be adopted? We know that, generally, adopted children do at least as well as other children in life, so adoption will not harm them but rather prevent them from a serious risk of abuse. But arguments such as these may be regarded as the first step down a slippery slope towards social engineering, whereby the state decides who will make a good parent. After all, is any parent entirely sure that there is no one else somewhere in the world who might make a better parent than them?

15

TO THE CARE HOME

CHOOSING WHEN AN ELDERLY PERSON should be placed in a care home is always difficult. No more so than in the next case we will look at. Mr and Mrs S married in 1945. They lived together for nearly fifty years. Mr S was, at the time of the case, ninety years old and Mrs S in her eighties. The central issue was straightforward: where should Mr S live? For Mrs S the answer was clear: he should remain with her. Although Mr S was no longer able to make decisions for himself, she felt able to care for him. However, the Primary Care Trust and local authority were not convinced that she was able to look after him and believed that Mr S should be placed in an EMI home. That is not some sort of musical establishment, but an Elderly Mentally Infirm home.

Mrs S accepted that she would need an extensive support package from the local authority if she were to be able to care for Mr S at their home. It was agreed that Mr S had profound needs, especially in relation to mobility and continence. As Mr Justice Charles put it, 'Mr S is a big man'.

Things came to a head on 10 September 2004 when Mr S had to be admitted to a nursing home. Mrs S admitted that she was getting desperate, given the lack of respite care from the local authority and their support for her generally. In a letter to the local authority she set out the history of her situation and explained that she was exhausted. She said that her blood pressure was rising and she could hardly walk. In capital letters she wrote 'PLEASE HELP'.

This led to the placing of Mr S in a nursing home. It is revealing that just five days later the nursing home informed the local authority that they could not cope with his care needs and behaviour. This gives an insight into what Mrs S was having to deal with. That she was able to care for a man that a team of younger, trained staff could not cope with is remarkable. Or looked at another way, that she was left without adequate respite care or support to look after a man that trained professionals were unable to look after is shocking. But what happens next?

After the problems at the nursing home, Mr S was placed in a hospital. On 21 September injunctions were obtained preventing Mrs S from removing Mr S from the hospital or even visiting it without the social service department's permission. These injunctions were obtained without notice to Mrs S. They indicate the extent to which the relationship between her and the social services department had deteriorated. No reason was given for the injunctions.

When social workers explained to her the impact of the court order Mrs S was described as being extremely distressed. She raised her voice and paced around the room. It is hardly surprising that a wife of nearly fifty years should react in this way when told that social workers would decide when and where she could see her husband. She was only allowed to see him when accompanied by a member of staff from the local authority. It was not until several months later that unsupervised contact was allowed.

In early 2005, following an order of the court, a trial return home was attempted with an agreed support package. That ended because Mr S became ill and had to be returned to hospital. The local authority wanted the court to confirm that they would determine where Mr S should live. Mrs S still wanted her husband returned to her.

The judge accepted that it was difficult to determine all of the facts of the case. The judge said emotions ran high: 'At times Mrs S would express herself in strong, demanding and emotional terms, sometimes justifiably and at other times with less (and sometimes no) justification. She had demonstrated ... a volatile and forceful side to her character.' The social worker dealing with the case said, 'It is like a roller-coaster all the time because she is a "this moment" person – she wants things to happen immediately. Although I do not think she realised it, it was like a care service just for Mr S and I suppose from her per-spective this is not unreasonable.'

It was not surprising that a major part of Mrs S's case was based on a claim that her human rights had been infringed. Mrs S sought to rely on a series of cases where the courts have considered the legality of local authorities removing babies from mothers at birth, on the basis that the mother poses a risk to their baby. The courts had held that there needs to be 'extra-ordinarily compelling' evidence if the removal of a baby in such a case is to be justified. Mrs S argued that the same test should be used for a couple who had been married a considerable length of time in considering whether to separate them. The anal-ogy was rejected by the judge. He maintained that the only test that needed to be satisfied was that the interference in their family life was necessary and proportionate. He felt that Mr S's need of expert care superseded his need of living with his wife.

Some might think that is a harsh approach to take. The relationship between a couple after a lengthy marriage will often be extremely close and it might seem that inadequate weight is attached to the significance of the relationship if the couple can be separated simply because it is judged to be in one of the parties' best interests that the couple are separated. Even if it was best for Mr S, and that seemed a rather borderline conclusion, it was not best for Mrs S. The court did not place any weight on her interests.

On the other hand, others will argue that Mr S's physical welfare, and the care he receives to maintain his health is of paramount importance. Many people who love each other dearly are separated when one has to have trained medical care, for example in rehabilitating from a spinal injury. The distress that Mr and Mrs S suffer in being separate is secondary to the expert care that can be provided for Mr S in a nursing home.

The court in this case relied on its 'inherent jurisdiction', that is, its right to take decisions on another's behalf. This originates not from a statute but from the essential power of the court to protect children and vulnerable adults. The latter phrase is rather undefined. Traditionally it was limited to those lacking mental capacity, but more recently has extended to other adults who have capacity, but are in some sense vulnerable. One judge explained:

"In the context of the inherent jurisdiction I would treat as a vulnerable adult someone who, whether or not mentally incapacitated, and whether or not suffering from any mental illness, or mental disorder, is or may be unable to take care of him or herself, or unable to protect him or herself against significant harm or exploitation, or who is deaf, blind, or dumb, or who is substantially handicapped by illness, injury or congenital deformity."

The inherent jurisdiction gives the courts wide power to protect people from harm. There are, however, real dangers with it. First, it could be used to interfere in a person's decisions about how they wish to live their life. In one case, for example, the local authority were concerned about a young woman with a variety of learning and other difficulties who had befriended a man who was generally regarded as not a good influence on her. For example, he encouraged her not to take medication and to ignore the advice of social workers. She had begun a sexual relationship with the man and the local authority sought to obtain orders to protect her from him. The wise judge hearing the case commented:

"The fact is that all life involves risk, and the young, the elderly and the vulnerable, are exposed to addi-

tional risks and to risks they are less well equipped than others to cope with. But just as wise parents resist the temptation to keep their children metaphorically wrapped up in cotton wool, so too we must avoid the temptation always to put the physical health and safety of the elderly and the vulnerable before everything else. Often it will be appropriate to do so, but not always. Physical health and safety can sometimes be bought at too high a price in happiness and emotional welfare. The emphasis must be on sensible risk appraisal, not striving to avoid all risk, whatever the price, but instead seeking a proper balance and being willing to tolerate manageable or acceptable risks as the price appropriately to be paid in order to achieve some other good – in particular to achieve the vital good of the elderly or vulnerable person's happiness. What good is it making someone safer if it merely makes them miserable?"

Most of us know people who are living their lives in ways we disapprove of or we think are harmful. We probably think we could live their lives in a better way. But we do not and should not be able to force them to live as we wish. It is a difficult judgment call for the courts to make, however, as they have duty to protect the vulnerable. They felt they were doing this in Mr S's case.

A second concern is that the inherent jurisdiction is just based on the best interests of the vulnerable person and does not place any weight on the interests of their family. One judge has even suggested that, although we have a strong presumption that children are best cared for by families, the law does not use the same presumption in relation to mentally incapacitated adults. The judge said that that would often be true, but it is not a formal legal presumption as it is in relation to children. Another judge seemed more willing to protect the interests of family members caring for a vulnerable adult. Judge Wood stated:

> *We should not lightly interfere with family life. If the State – typically, as here, in the guise of a local authority – is to say that it is the more appropriate person to look after a mentally incapacitated adult than her own partner or family, it assumes, as it seems to me, the burden – not the legal burden but the practical and evidential burden – of establishing that this is indeed so.*

Such an approach might also find support with reference to Article 8 of the European Convention on Human Rights, which protects the right to respect for private and family life. Indeed, it might be argued that a mere assumption is all an adequate protection of Article 8 requires. Certainly this is an area where local authorities need clearer guidance from Parliament as to what powers they have and what obligations too.

All theory aside, let's return to the case of Mr and Mrs S. The court confirmed that the local authority had the power to determine where Mr S was to live and to forcibly separate a loving couple who had been married for nearly fifty years. While they felt they had Mr S's best interests at heart, this whole sad situation might have been avoided if a more effective regime of care and support had been put in place earlier for the couple. An ounce of prevention is worth a pound of cure, as the saying goes.

Too often individuals are left to care for frail older people without sufficient help and recognition from the state and the wider community. Leaving them without assistance, only to rush in when it is too late seems an inadequate response, and probably more expensive as well. As the number of older people is set to rise in our society we need to be much more imaginative in thinking about their care and supporting those who look after them. We'll all be old one day, if we're lucky enough to make it, so let's get this one right.